homeChef
Neven Maguire

homeChef
Neven Maguire

Collins

This book is dedicated to my mother, Vera, who gave me her love and appreciation for food. I'll be forever grateful.

This paperback edition published in 2011
First published in 2009 by Collins

HarperCollins Publishers
77–85 Fulham Palace Road,
London, W6 8JB
www.harpercollins.co.uk

A catalogue record for this book is available from the British Library.

ISBN 978–0–00–741933–3

Editorial Director: Jenny Heller
Project Editor: Ione Walder
Copy Editor: Jane Bamforth
Photography: David Munns
Food and Styling: Bridget Sargeson and Sue Rowlands
Design: Nicky Barneby and Steve Boggs

INPRODUCTION

The TV series *Home Chef* was produced and directed by David Hare, (InProduction) in association with Bord Bia.
Recipes from the series can also be found at **www.nevenmaguire.com**

The author and publishers would like to thank Belleek (www.belleek.ie) and Figgjo (www.figgjo.no), who kindly donated chinaware for the photography.

Colour reproduction by Butler Tanner & Dennis, Frome, Somerset
Printed and bound in China

Contents

Introduction

The work involved in producing a book is always exciting. But this one has been especially important for me. I have now had 32 happy years in this world and have been cooking professionally for half of them. I have enjoyed every minute and cannot imagine any other life except that of being a chef. That is the kernel of this book. The aim of *Home Chef* is to help give people the confidence to cook at a high level in their own home, from everyday family meals to dishes with a generous helping of the 'wow' factor.

When I think back to my early training days, I realise how my cooking has changed over the years and how the knowledge of my customers has developed. There are many people out there who are deeply interested in food and wine and very knowledgeable about what they eat and how it is prepared. Sometimes, diners in the restaurant tell me about meals where they each cooked a different course from my previous books. It is always interesting to hear how people use my books and so it is vital that my recipes are tried and tested to ensure that people get real pleasure from the results. I had these cooks very much in mind when deciding on material for *Home Chef* and developing recipes that would produce good results for readers. I hope this book will work well for everyone.

I remember my first week in catering college: I cut vegetables for the entire time, forcing me to learn knife skills before cooking a single thing. As a result, I've included in this book the bits of information that I think of as the building blocks of good cooking – what to look for when buying knives, what to keep in your larder, and essential skills such as filleting fish. I want *Home Chef* to be a one-stop resource to help readers know what to request from their butcher, local growers, or at the farmers market. There is also a chapter full of sauces and dressings that you can make, keep, freeze and then use when needed. With so many people cooking at home, this will help them to buy in and prepare ahead.

No one wants to be stuck in the kitchen all day – that's my job! Guests at the restaurant want a memorable meal. They don't just want a piece of beef – they want it cooked in four different ways. This is okay for me with nine chefs in the kitchen, but no good for the home cook. I have given the recipes a lot of thought so that you can manage the dishes at home and at the same time flex your culinary muscles. I hope this is a book that you will keep on coming back to and get good use from over the years. What I really want is for everyone to cook something really delicious to eat with family and friends. If *Home Chef* helps you to do this, I will be well satisfied.

Happy Cooking!

Using This Book

There are recipes in this book for all abilities and I've tried to include ways for more confident cooks to stretch their skills a little further. The level of each recipe is shown by the number of chef's hats beside it:

⚐ Straightforward

⚐⚐ Intermediate

⚐⚐⚐ Stretch your Skills Further

If you're nervous about trying some of the more advanced recipes, you can always make just the main part of the dish, and save the accompaniments or sauces for when you've had a bit more experience. Don't forget to refer to the glossary on pages 34–6 if there are words or phrases that you're not familiar with.

Oven Temperatures Timings and temperatures are given for fan ovens. If you're using a conventional oven, increase the temperature by 10 degrees.

Eggs All recipes were tested using medium-sized eggs (size 3). Try to use free-range or organic eggs wherever possible. Look out for the Bord Bia Quality Assurance mark; in the UK, look out for the Lion Quality mark.

Herbs Unless otherwise stated, all herbs used in the recipes are fresh.

Chef's Skills

Store Cupboard Essentials

One of the best-kept secrets of the clever cook is a well-stocked larder. From basic essentials such as eggs and milk to handy convenience foods like Mexican flour tortillas, if you keep yourself well organised, you'll never run short of ideas when it comes to preparing tasty food. Of course, I have many items in my store cupboards, some of which you might not need, so either omit them or swap them for similar items that you prefer – after all, cookery is all about experimentation and personal taste.

Whatever you do decide to put in it, keep your store cupboard tidy – regularly throw out items that are out of date and arrange things logically. I always put little stickers on the tops of my spice jars so that I can find the one I want without having to rifle through every single jar. Try to buy spices in small quantities as ideally they should be replenished every six months or so.

Canned foods

Chopped plum tomatoes

Sweetcorn kernels

Chickpeas

Coconut milk (I buy all my oriental ingredients from a company called Thai Gold. They are available by mail order and in Irish supermarkets)

Tuna

Anchovies

Black olives

Baked beans

Fresh goods

Spring onions

Tomatoes

Garlic

Onions

Potatoes

Celery

Carrots

Oranges and lemons

Bread: soft flour tortillas; sliced bread; longer-life part-baked breads such as Italian ciabatta

Bottles and jars

Sunflower oil

Olive oil

Extra virgin olive oil

Toasted sesame oil

Duck/goose fat

White wine and red wine vinegar

Balsamic vinegar

Soy sauce (light and dark)

Tomato ketchup

Wholegrain and Dijon mustard

Worcestershire sauce

Tabasco sauce

Sweet chilli sauce

Thai fish sauce (nam pla)

Sun-dried tomato paste

Tomato purée

Roasted red peppers

Horseradish sauce

Capers

Mayonnaise

Clear honey

Nutella

Toffee sauce

Jam

Vanilla extract (not essence)

Wine: red; white; sherry; port; brandy

In the fridge

Milk

Eggs

Butter

Double cream, crème fraîche and Greek yoghurt

Mascarpone cheese

Parmesan

Mature Cheddar

Smoked streaky bacon

Parma ham

Wild rocket

Chilli Jam (for homemade, see page 215)

Red Onion Marmalade (for homemade, see page 209)

Port and Balsamic Syrup (for homemade, see page 214)

In the freezer

As well as buying ready-frozen items, I like to freeze these handy time-savers:

Root ginger: much easier to grate when frozen. Peel 2.5cm (1in) pieces and wrap in freezer film before freezing

Herbs: leftover fresh herbs can be put in strong plastic bags and stored in the freezer. They're ready for cooking with at any time, so when you need them, just pull off a handful and crumble into the pan – no need to chop

Bread: most bread freezes very well, particularly in individual slices ready for putting straight into the toaster

Stock: freeze stocks in 600ml (1 pint) rigid plastic containers and allow to thaw before using

Galangal, kaffir lime leaves and curry leaves: freeze any leftovers in small strong plastic bags and use straight from the freezer

Garden peas

Vanilla ice cream

Pastry: puff, shortcrust, filo and kataifi (for more info see pages 70 and 216)

Spring roll wrappers

Wonton wrappers

Dried goods

Baking powder

Bicarbonate of soda

Flours: plain, strong plain, self-raising and wholemeal

Dried yeast sachets

Spaghetti

Pasta shapes e.g. penne / tagliatelle (I prefer the De Cecco brand)

Egg noodles

Rice: long grain, basmati, risotto and organic brown

Couscous

White beans, such as haricot

Polenta

Dried mixed wild mushrooms

Popcorn kernels

Digestive biscuits

Plain chocolate (at least 70% cocoa solids)

Sugar: caster, light muscovado and icing

Stock cubes (The Kallo brand are good and also low in salt)

Maldon sea salt

Herbs and spices: black peppercorns, ground cumin, coriander, paprika, cinnamon, Chinese five-spice, cayenne, dried chilli flakes, curry powder and paste, cloves, saffron and vanilla pods

Dried fruit: raisins/sultanas, apricots, prunes

Nuts: flaked almonds, pine nuts and pecan nuts

Sesame seeds

Fresh Herbs

Herbs contribute hugely to my enjoyment of food. I use them to add scent, flavour and colour to almost every dish that I produce in the kitchen. It's hard to imagine cooking without them. The flavour of each herb comes from the essential oils stored in its leaves, stems and flowers, which are released as the leaf is cut, torn or heated. To illustrate this, pick a leaf of basil, sage or tarragon and crush between your fingers. Notice how much more pungent and powerful the smell becomes. I'd like to say I grow all my own herbs, but I am lucky enough to have two local organic growers who deliver to me regularly. They pick the herbs at about 6.30am, when the plants are holding the most moisture. However, I do grow some mint in the garden and always have a pot of basil on the windowsill in my kitchen. Always add chopped herbs right at the end of the cooking or they will discolour and their flavour may change. I keep herbs in a bowl of water until the last minute to prevent them wilting.

Basil

No other herb brings the flavour of Mediterranean cooking into your kitchen in quite the same way. Its warm, spicy smell and flavour livens up a tomato salad, or it can be pounded with Parmesan, pine nuts and olive oil to make pesto (see page 208). If you are using it raw, it is better to shred the leaves by hand as this helps retain the flavour. There are several varieties: sweet, which I cook with; purple for garnishing; Napolina, which has leaves nearly the size of your hand and is best for pesto; and Thai holy basil (basil in name only, as not technically from the same family), which is perfect in oriental dishes.

Bay leaves

The strong and distinctive flavour of bay is best released by lengthy cooking. It is part of the classic bouquet garni. We use bay leaves in court-bouillon (see page 34), stocks (see pages 218–19), casseroles and pot roasts.

Chervil

Its delicate anise flavour is ideal in salads, soups, stews and sauces. Use in any recipe calling for 'fines herbes', and with white meat. Excellent in herb butter. Avoid prolonged cooking as this destroys the flavour and colour.

Chives

Use in dressings, as a garnish or chop into summer salads. The flowers look great in salads. Chives are essential in potato salad and can be used in egg dishes or to flavour butter for barbecuing. They tend to discolour, so add at the very end of cooking. Onion- and garlic-flavoured chives are also available.

Coriander

Use in Middle Eastern and Asian dishes. It's especially good scattered on top of curries, and is best added towards the end of cooking. The roots and stalks can also be ground down and used in curry pastes and marinades.

Dill

This has a mild caraway flavour and is best added just before serving. Use in fish marinades, sauces, soups and salads. I also find it particularly good with potatoes, chicken, fish and egg recipes.

Marjoram

This has pungent leaves and flowers. Hang small bunches in a warm, dry place to dry out, then store in labelled screw-topped jars in a dark cupboard and use in homemade tomato sauces or to flavour tomato pulp for pizzas. Marjoram makes a good addition to a marinade, particularly for fish. We use fresh marjoram in the restaurant as part of our special herbal tea – a wonderful mixture of bronze fennel, apple mint, lemon thyme, lemon balm and marjoram. The tea aids digestion and has the most fantastic fragrance.

Mint

Many flavours of mint are available, including peppermint, ginger, apple and pineapple. Toss with new potatoes or peas, or serve as a sauce with roast lamb. It is wonderful in summer drinks and fruit salads or serve with ice cream and your favourite summer berries. We serve freshly brewed mint and peppermint tea in the restaurant and both are very popular.

Parsley

There are two kinds of parsley: curly parsley and the continental flat-leaf parsley. Both have a vivid green colour and although the continental variety has a more pronounced flavour, they can be used interchangeably in almost any savoury recipe. Parsley is the most used herb in my kitchen. Finely chop with garlic and mix with butter to put on top of mussels, to flavour grilled meat or fish, or simply to mix with vegetables.

I. Basil

2. Chervil

3. Chives

4. Coriander

5. Dill

6. Marjoram

7. Sage

8. Rosemary

9. Tarragon

Rocket (common or wild)

This old-fashioned salad herb is enjoying a great revival. It has a spicy flavour and makes an excellent simple salad or can be quickly cooked in a little olive oil. In Italy it is often served with carpaccio: thin slices of raw beef with Parmesan shavings and a dribble of olive oil (see page 92) but it is equally good with slices of smoked salmon.

Rosemary

A very strongly flavoured herb, so use sparingly. It's often finely chopped in stuffing for poultry, meat and game. I also like to insert sprigs into roast lamb or pork – remove them before serving. Occasionally we use rosemary in sweet dishes such as creams, custards or poached fruit (such as pears).

Sage

Not subtle, but very versatile, this can be used fresh or dried and is excellent combined with tomatoes, olive oil and garlic. It works well with fatty meats like pork or duck, or, as is traditional in Italy, with offal such as kidneys and liver. Some of the best stuffed pasta dishes of the Italian Modena region are served simply with melted butter and sage leaves.

Tarragon

Its delicate aniseed flavour goes well with chicken. Considered by the French as one of the most important culinary herbs, this is an essential ingredient of béarnaise sauce. A few sprigs make a nice addition to pot-roasted chicken, or infuse in vinegar to make a vinaigrette.

Thyme

One of the most important and widely used herbs, which comes in a variety of flavours. It has an intensely aromatic flavour, perfect in slow-cooked dishes, such as casseroles. Thyme is an ingredient of the bouquet garni, together with parsley and bay. A couple of sprigs of lemon thyme work well tucked into a whole salmon or trout, or try stuffing the cavity of a roast duck with orange thyme.

Equip Yourself

The first step to becoming a successful home chef is to keep your kitchen well equipped. You don't need a lot of gear, but it makes sense to buy the best you can afford, then you know it will work for you and last a decent amount of time. Below left are the essential items that everyone should own, while the handy extras on the right are things I use less often. You might choose to buy only some of these, but I like to have them all to hand as they save me time and effort and help me to create stunning results.

The Basics

1 large sharp knife (Cook's knife)

1 small sharp knife (Paring knife)

1 bread knife

1 chef's steel/knife sharpener

Can opener

2 chopping boards

Large non-stick frying pan

3 sizes of heavy-based saucepans

3 wooden spoons (or I use heatproof Mafter exoglass spoons)

Set of kitchen scales

Colander

Measuring jug

Metal hand whisk

Metal sieve

Slotted spoon

Fish slice

Potato masher

Swivel-style vegetable peeler

Box-style cheese grater

Pastry brush

Rolling pin

Roasting tin

Baking sheet

Casserole dish with lid

Tiered bamboo steamer

Cast-iron griddle pan (with metal handle)

Handy Extras

Lemon zester

Lemon juicer

Tongs

Tweezers (for boning fish)

Potato ricer

Palette knife

Hand-held blender (my preference is Bamix)

Food processor

Kitchen scissors

Wok

Rubber spatula (heatproof)

Flour dredger

Chef's blowtorch

Nylon sieve (for straining fruit, as some fruits react with metal)

Mortar and pestle

Measuring spoons

6 ramekins (try to build up a selection of different sizes)

6 dariole moulds (castle-shaped ramekins, narrower at one end)

Microplane grater (try to build up a selection of different blades)

Fluted round cutters (in various sizes)

Chef's rings – 10cm (4in), 6cm (2½in) and 5cm (2in)

Disposable piping bags and nozzles

23cm (9in) loose-bottomed cake tin

Muffin tin and mini-muffin tin

Knives

Although you can get by with just the three knives listed on page 17, a full set of good knives is the best investment a keen cook can ever make. I recommend buying the most expensive set of knives you can possibly afford, because they should last for the rest of your life. I use Henckel knives, which are available from most good cookware shops, department stores and online.

When choosing a knife set, one of the most important factors to consider is the type of steel used to make the blades. The majority of knives are manufactured from a blend of high-carbon stainless steel that resists rust and corrosion and is dishwasher-proof. The 'tang' is the part of the knife where the metal is attached to the handle. The best knives will have a tang in which the metal visibly extends inside the handle, right to the end.

Good-quality knives are well balanced and feel good in the cook's hand. Don't be afraid to try holding them in the shop. They should be easy to handle and should feel solid, not flimsy. As a general rule, a good knife should feel like an extension of your own hand and should allow adequate space between the point where your fingers grip the knife and the surface on to which you are cutting. Once a month, we get someone to come into the restaurant to sharpen our knives, but a good butcher should be happy to do this for you – they normally have machines which will do a good job in seconds. You can also sharpen the knives yourself using a sharpening steel (see page 21 for instructions).

If you do decide to invest in a set of knives, the ones listed overleaf are the basic set with which I would begin. It's also worth getting a knife block so that the knives can be kept in a safe place and are easily accessible. It helps prevent them from getting damaged or ruined.

1. Sharpening steel

2. Paring knife

3. Cook's knife

4. Bread knife

Cook's Knife

This is the knife I use most often and which I could never do without in the kitchen. Its 26cm (10½in) blade gives me the perfect balance between handle and blade, allowing excellent hold – perfect for chopping vegetables or herbs.

Carving Knife

To ensure the perfect edge for carving meat, poultry, etc., choose a carving knife with a long, thin and slightly upturned blade.

Boning Knife

An authentic butcher's knife, designed especially to separate meat from bone. The blade is characteristically thin and curved, which ensures a thin cut. It can be used to remove the bones and cuts through meat very easily.

Bread Knife

This knife has a long serrated blade of approximately 20cm (8in). A good one will slice bread without leaving a lot of crumbs.

Scalloped Slicing Knife

A perfect knife for slicing roasts and dense meats such as large continental sausages. It has a comfortable handle and the scallops on the blade trap small air bubbles between the metal and the food, preventing the food from sticking to the blade and making it easy to slice meats very finely. The scalloped slicing knife is also good for cutting thicker slices with more precision. However, it is not suitable for carving meat on the bone – it's too long and doesn't have a point, so will feel very clumsy in this situation.

Filleting Knife

Despite its name, which suggests it is used for meat, this knife's speciality is actually fish! Choose one with a thin, flexible blade for performing the most delicate kitchen operation: preparing perfect fillets. You'll also need tweezers to remove the last few tiny bones left in the fillet.

Paring Knife

Used to trim meat and remove lard, fat and sinew, and to peel and cut up fruits and vegetables. A paring knife has a blade approximately 10cm (4in) long that allows you to work easily. You can also buy ones with a serrated edge, which stay sharper for longer and the tops don't tend to break off.

Sharpening Steel

An essential accessory for keeping your knives sharp. Hold the steel vertically, either pressed on to a tea towel on a flat surface as shown below, or, when you feel more confident, held freely at arm's length in front of you. Slide the knife blade down the steel, at an angle, then again down the opposite side of the steel. Repeat about six times on each side until the knife is sharp – your cutting edge is now ready for work.

Knife Skills for Fish

Cleaning Round Fish *(for when serving whole)*
Such as cod, haddock, trout, salmon and sea bass

Snip the fins off the fish with kitchen scissors and then remove the scales by scraping the fish from head to tail with a blunt, thick-bladed knife. To remove the guts, slit open the belly from the anal fin (two-thirds of the way down the fish from the head) up towards the head. Pull out most of the guts with your hand, then cut away any entrails left behind and wash out the cavity under cold running water.

Cleaning Flat Fish *(for when serving whole)*
Such as sole and plaice

To remove the guts, locate the gut cavity by pressing on the whitest side of the fish just below the head until you find an area that is much softer. Make a small incision across this area and pull out the guts with your little finger. Trim the fish by snipping off the fins with kitchen scissors.

Filleting Round Fish

Lay the fish on the board and, on the uppermost side, cut closely around the head in a V-shape so that you don't lose too much of the fillet. Lay the fish with its back towards you (unless you are left-handed like me, in which case place it with its back away from you). Cut along the length of the back, keeping the blade of the knife above the horizontal backbone.

Starting at the head, cut the fillet away from the bones, keeping the blade as close to them as you can. Once you have released some of the fillet, lift it up with your fingers to make it easier to see where you are cutting. When you near the rib bones, cut as close to them as you can or, if very fine, cut through them and then remove the bones from the fillet afterwards using tweezers.

Turn the fish over, again cut the V-shape around the head, and repeat the rest of the cuts to remove the fillet from the second side.

Filleting Flat Fish

You will get four fillets from a flat fish. Lay the fish on a chopping board and cut around the back of the head and also across the tail. »

1. Filleting round fish: cut V-shape

2. Cut down the length of the back

3. Cut the fillet away from the bone

4. Remove the fillet and turn over

5. Repeat same cuts on the other side

6. Two perfect fillets from round fish

7. Filleting flat fish: cut around head

8. Cut down the centre of the fish

9. Fold back the fillet as you cut

Then cut through the skin down the centre of the fish, very slightly to one side of the raised backbone, working from the head down to the tail.

Starting where the backbone meets the head, slide the blade of the knife under the corner of one of the fillets. Carefully cut away from the bones, folding the released fillet back as you do so. Keep the blade of the knife almost flat and as close to the bones as possible. Remove the adjacent fillet in the same way. Turn the fish over and repeat on the other side.

Skinning Fillets of Fish

Place the fillet skin-side down on a chopping board with the narrowest (tail) end nearest to you. Angling the blade of the knife down towards the skin, start to cut between the flesh and the skin until a little flap is released.

Flip the fish over. Firmly take hold of the skin and, working away from you, continue to cut between the flesh and skin, sawing with the knife from side to side and keeping the blade of the knife close against the skin until all the skin is removed.

Preparing Prawns or Langoustines
Including tiger and Dublin Bay

Firmly twist the head away from the body and discard, or rinse and keep to use for stock (see page 219). Lay the prawn upside-down and break open the shell along the belly, then carefully peel the shell away from the flesh.

With large, raw prawns it is important to remove the intestinal tract, which looks like a thin black vein running down the back of the prawn flesh. Run the tip of a small knife down the back of the prawn and then lift up and pull out the vein.

Preparing Vegetables

Always shake or brush off any loose earth before washing vegetables. All vegetables must be thoroughly washed before cooking, with the exception of mushrooms, which should be brushed or wiped using a pastry brush. As cultivated mushrooms are grown in sterile soil this is sufficient. If they are genuinely wild, then trim them down, cutting off any bruised or damaged bits with a small, pointed knife, and brush or wipe as before.

Vegetables with inedible skins (such as onion, thick-skinned roots and tubers, and some squashes) need to be peeled. A vegetable peeler or small paring knife is best for peeling. A really sharp knife (see pages 20–1) and a good, heavy chopping board are essential for slicing and chopping.

Some vegetables, notably celeriac, artichoke bottoms, Jerusalem artichokes and salsify, rapidly discolour and begin to lose their vitamins once they are cut. To prevent this, try not to prepare them too far in advance. When peeling and cutting the vegetables, use a stainless steel knife and drop them immediately into 'acidulated' water. To prepare acidulated water, simply add the juice of one lemon to 600ml (1 pint) water.

How to Peel Garlic

Cut the root end off the clove of garlic. Lay the clove flat on the chopping board and rest the blade of a large knife horizontally on it. Lean heavily on the flat blade with the heel of your hand. The garlic clove will crack under the weight and will simultaneously be released from its papery skin. Remove any green stalk from the centre and finely chop using a rocking motion.

How to Chop an Onion

Peel the onion and chop off the root and tip. (If you're less confident, you can leave the root attached until the last minute to hold the pieces securely together. But don't forget to remove it before cooking!) Cut the onion in half through the root end (see the step by step pictures over the page). Place one half of the onion flat-side down on the chopping board. »

Make about six parallel cuts downwards with the knife tip pointing towards the root end, but cutting short of the root end so that the onion continues to hold together.

Next, with the onion still facing downwards, and holding it steady from the root end, make three horizontal cuts one above the other, towards the root. Again, be careful not to slice all the way through – the half must still hold together.

Finally, chop down repeatedly across the width of the onion. Perfect cubes will fall from your knife!

Using a Mandolin

A mandolin is a plane-slicer tool, which originated in the Far East and is used to cut potatoes or other vegetables. Most models offer various cuts and thicknesses but typically they have three blades – one each for fine, medium and large ribbons. If you haven't used a mandolin before, try to purchase one that has a tripod and a guard for your fingers.

Julienne

This is a term used when vegetables or fruit rind are cut into very fine strips. Peel the skin from the vegetable if necessary. Trim away any root or stem parts. If the vegetable is round, like a potato or carrot, cut in half and lay it cut-side down on the board. This will keep it from rolling. Cut the edible part of the vegetable into slices about 3mm (⅛in) thick. Cut around the seeds and discard if necessary. Turn these slices on their side and slice again into even strips 3mm (⅛in) thick. Use as required.

Brunoise

Brunoise is a method of chopping in which the vegetable is first julienned (see above) and then turned 90 degrees and sliced again, producing cubes or dice with a side length of no more than 3mm (⅛in). The cubes should be consistent in size and shape, to create an attractive finish. Common vegetables to be brunoised are leeks, turnips and carrots. The diced vegetables are blanched briefly in salty boiling water and then submerged in ice water for a few seconds to set the colour. The brunoise is often used as a garnish – for example, scattered on a consommé (a type of soup).

Choosing Meat

A good butcher is invaluable; a shop run by helpful, knowledgeable staff inevitably means they care about the meat they stock and will have treated it properly. They should be able to advise you about cooking times and recommended methods as well as prepare joints and steaks to your requirements.

Meat should always look and smell fresh. A bright red or pink doesn't necessarily indicate freshness. Instead, look for a good, clear colour; although bear in mind that it will darken naturally on exposure to air. Beef should be well hung for a better flavour. Look out for labels stating that the meat has been 'dry aged'. This means that 30 per cent of the moisture has been removed and as a result the beef should be firm to the touch.

Any fat should be creamy white; if it's yellow (except for some very specialist breeds), the meat is probably past its prime. Look for a smooth outer layer of fat, if appropriate to the cut, and a fair amount of 'marbled' fat distributed throughout the meat; this will keep it moist during cooking and add flavour.

Always look for a neat, well-trimmed piece of meat, with sinew removed. Splinters of bone and ragged edges indicate poor butchery. Joints and steaks should be of uniform thickness so that they cook evenly.

Minced meat is best eaten on the day of purchase. Larger joints, chops and steaks will keep for 2–3 days. Lean cuts will keep for longer as it is the fat that turns rancid first. If in doubt, smell it – 'off' meat will have an unpleasant odour and a slimy surface.

I always remove meat from its original wrapping and then put it, wrapped in fresh cling film, on a plate in the fridge to prevent blood dripping through the fridge shelves. Remember to always store raw meat away from cooked foods to prevent cross-contamination. As a general rule, remove meat from the fridge 30 minutes to 1 hour before you intend to use it. This allows it to relax and return to room temperature. Once cooked, rest it once more so that the juices stay in the meat after it is cut. »

In Ireland we are lucky enough to have a Quality Assurance scheme run by Bord Bia, the Irish food board, who are committed to supporting Irish farmers and the industry to produce the safest and highest quality food possible. Bord Bia have tirelessly championed Irish meat abroad and have been responsible for allowing artisan businesses to blossom and expand under their watchful eye. Look out for their quality mark – a shamrock with an Irish flag. It guarantees that the meat can be traced back to the farm on which the animal was reared.

Meal Planning

There are many factors to consider when planning a menu and it may seem a difficult and daunting task, especially when tackling it for the first time. Begin by thinking about the people you are cooking for and what type of dishes they might enjoy. I like to give people one ingredient that perhaps they haven't tried before. However, it is important to think about availability, to make sure that you don't spend too much time running about trying to find particular ingredients. Always check the dietary requirements of your guests to make sure that you are catering for everyone. That said, I often make an extra dish or two, just in case there's an allergy or food dislike that I'm not aware of.

For the best flavour, choose your dishes based on seasonality; if you are unsure, visit your local farmers' market and ask the growers what produce is at its best.

Think about which dishes can be made in advance or even prepared and frozen beforehand. When entertaining at home I aim to have at least one course made in advance – usually the dessert. Many dishes can also be prepared up to a certain stage and then kept covered in the fridge until needed. Just make sure that you allow everything to come back to room temperature before cooking or serving it.

Try to get a good balance in your menu and avoid overlap ingredients. It is also important not to make too many of the dishes overly rich and heavy; although they will be delicious, your guests will start to struggle. »

Devise a time plan for the evening and make a note of how long different things need in the oven. This stops you from becoming flustered once your guests arrive and allows you to enjoy the evening and take part in the chat!

If you are nervous, perhaps try out the dishes on close friends and family first. The less pressure you have on your shoulders the better, and the more likely everyone is to have a good night. Once you have mastered a dish, then you can build on it and take it to the next level. The most important thing to remember when entertaining is to relax and enjoy it!

10 Chef's Tricks

Like anything else, cooking takes patience and practice. Even though I've been cooking for years, I'm always discovering new ways to make my job that little bit easier, or working out how to fix things when they go wrong. Here are ten of my most useful tips and secrets.

- If you taste a casserole, soup or sauce and it is too salty, try adding a handful of raw potato cubes, and allow them to cook over a gentle heat. They will soak up the excess salt and can then be removed with a slotted spoon before serving.

- To get the fat to separate instantly from delicious roasting juices, add a handful of ice cubes, then quickly skim off the fat that rises to the top. This method works best if you pour the juices into a heatproof jug first.

- Cover large joints of meat with foil, shiny side inwards, before cooking to prevent them from over-browning while in the oven.

- I normally fry meat and fish in a mixture of oil and butter as the butter gives flavour and the oil stops the butter from burning.

- If your homemade mayonnaise begins to split or curdle, try adding a tablespoon of warm water and give it a good whisk.

- If a béchamel sauce becomes lumpy, simply blitz with a hand-held blender until smooth.

♟ Once cooked, quickly refresh pasta under cold running water to prevent further cooking. This is particularly important when making a pasta salad or gratin.

♟ To prevent a pastry case from shrinking away from the sides of the tin while cooking, try to leave the pastry-lined tin in the fridge for at least 30 minutes before putting in the oven. It is also worth being gentle when rolling out, and don't overstretch the pastry when lining the tin.

♟ When blind baking pastry, I prefer to use foil to line the case rather than baking paper, because you end up with a more even light golden finish. Lightly oil the shiny side of the foil, place it oiled side down on to the pastry and fill with baking beans. Bake for 15–20 minutes.

♟ To make your own vanilla sugar, rinse any used vanilla pods and stick into a jar of caster sugar, then set aside for a couple of weeks before using. (I always buy my vanilla from a website called www.vanillabazaar.com.)

Glossary

Have you ever come across a cooking instruction that you're not sure about? There are so many terms and techniques in cooking, and not all recipes explain them in detail. But don't be put off cooking a dish because the recipe uses specialist language – in this glossary I've explained some of the most important words and phrases that you'll need to know.

Al Dente The texture of properly cooked pasta, vegetables and risottos. Literally 'to the tooth' (in Italian), it describes the slight resistance in the food when bitten.

Baste To spoon or brush a liquid (such as dripping from the pan, butter, fats or a marinade) over foods during roasting or grilling, to keep moist.

Blanch To parboil by immersing in rapidly boiling water for a few seconds or minutes. Normally used for vegetables such as French beans, sugar snap peas and mangetout. This helps to retain colour and flavour.

Braise A slow cooking method used for cuts of meat that are too tough to roast. It is also good for some vegetables. A pan or casserole with a tight-fitting lid should be used so that very little liquid is lost through evaporation. The meat is first browned, then cooked on a bed of roughly chopped vegetables (often called a 'mirepoix'), with just enough liquid to cover the vegetables. It can be cooked in the oven or on the hob.

Caramelise To heat (under a grill, in a pan or using a chef's blowtorch) so that the natural sugars in the food burn slightly and go brown. Sugar can also be sprinkled on food to create this effect, as in crème brulée.

Coulis Fruit that is sweetened with sugar and thinned with water, then puréed to form a fruit sauce or decoration for desserts.

Court-bouillon Flavoured liquid used for poaching fish. Made from water and wine or wine vinegar, with herbs and vegetables for flavouring.

Dauphinoise To cook 'à la Dauphinoise' means to bake in a slow oven with cream and garlic. A gratin dauphinoise is a classic dish of thinly sliced potatoes cooked with garlic, cream, milk, butter and often Gruyère cheese – rich, but delicious! Serve alongside meat or vegetable dishes.

Deglaze To loosen the sediment from the bottom of a pan by heating a little stock, wine or other liquid, along with cooking juices left in the pan after roasting or sautéing meat, and stirring with a wooden spoon.

Dice To cut into very small cubes of similar size and shape.

Dredge To coat food with flour or another powdered ingredient.

Flambé To flavour a dish with alcohol, usually brandy or rum, which is then ignited so that the actual alcohol content is burnt off, leaving the flavour behind. This can be done with a lighter, although chefs tend to simply tilt the pan and use the flame of the gas! Take great care!!

Fold To gently blend two mixtures, releasing as little air as possible. Cut through the mixture with a spatula or whisk, from bottom to top, rotating the bowl constantly, until thoroughly mixed.

Fondant A classic, restaurant method of cooking potato, producing a deliciously rich and buttery potato dish. Also a baked dessert which is cake-like on the outside but soft in the centre.

Gelatine An unflavoured substance that gives body to mousses and desserts, and aids setting. Available in leaves or powdered form. Traditional forms are not suitable for vegetarians, though some versions now are. A good alternative is agar agar, which is now more widely available from good health food shops. Simply follow the instructions on the packet.

Hull To remove the tough part of fruit under the stalk (e.g. strawberries).

Marinade / To Marinate A marinade is an acidic-based liquid mixture combining various seasonings, used to flavour and tenderise (particularly meat). To marinate meat, either brush food with the mixture or immerse in it and leave for at least 1–3 hours but preferably overnight.

Poach To cook very gently in liquid kept just below boiling point.

Purée To mash until perfectly smooth, either by hand, by pushing through a sieve or by mixing in a food processor or liquidiser.

Reduce To simmer liquid without a lid until much of the moisture evaporates and the sauce has thickened.

Refresh To dip into cold water or run cold water over food that has been parboiled or 'blanched' in hot water. This stops food from cooking any further and keeps a good colour.

Rind Thin outer coloured layer of a citrus fruit's skin. Can be removed with a special zester, a vegetable peeler or a box grater. Also the outer skin on bacon or cheese, which is normally removed.

Sauté To cook gently in a small amount of oil and butter in a pan over a low heat. The butter gives the flavour and the oil prevents it from burning. Also used to give the food a nice golden brown colour.

Seal To brown food very quickly on all sides to seal in juices and flavour, and to improve appearance and colour.

Seasoning A mixture of three parts salt to one part ground black pepper.

Simmer To keep a liquid or sauce at a point just below boiling, so that small bubbles rise slowly to the surface, breaking before they reach it.

Sweat To cook slowly in oil, butter or a mixture of both.

Syrup Sugar dissolved in liquid (usually water) over a medium heat.

Wilt To cook until limp, especially soft leaf vegetables such as spinach, rocket and pak choi.

Bread

MacNean White Bread

Makes two 450g (1lb) loaves

700g (1½lb) strong unbleached white flour, plus extra for dusting

2 x 7g sachets of easy blend dried yeast

25g (1oz) caster sugar

1 tsp salt

olive oil, for oiling

1 egg beaten with 1 tbsp water

butter, to serve

We serve this bread in the restaurant at the start of every meal. The basic recipe can be adapted in many ways – try adding to the dough up to 10 tablespoons of chopped fresh mixed soft herbs, such as flat-leaf parsley, basil and chives. Or add 4 tablespoons of Sun-dried Tomato Pesto (see page 208) along with a teaspoon of fennel seeds. Alternatively, spread the dough with Red Onion Marmalade (see page 209) before cooking.

You can make the dough in a food mixer or by hand. To make in a food mixer, place the flour in the bowl of the machine, and use the the dough hook attachment. Add the yeast, 450ml (16fl oz) lukewarm water, sugar and salt. Switch on the machine and mix until you have a very sloppy dough. Then knead on medium speed for 6–8 minutes until the dough becomes slightly sticky but pliable.

Alternatively, to make the bread by hand, place the flour in a large mixing bowl. Add the yeast, 450ml (16fl oz) lukewarm water, sugar and salt and mix with your fingers for 2–3 minutes to incorporate the flour, scraping the sides of the bowl and folding the dough over itself until it gathers into a rough mass. Turn out on to a well-floured work surface; lightly flour your hands. Knead for 6–8 minutes using the heel of your hand, until the dough is smooth and pliable. The dough will be very sticky at first; keep your hands and the work surface lightly floured, using a dough scraper if necessary to prevent it from sticking and building up on the work surface. As you continue kneading, the dough will become more elastic and easier to handle.

Shape the dough into a loose ball, then place in an oiled bowl and cover with cling film. Leave to rise for 1 hour until doubled in size.

Lightly oil two 450g (1lb) loaf tins. Knock back the risen dough by punching it lightly with a clenched fist to knock out trapped bubbles, then turn it out again on to a lightly floured surface and knead for 2–3 minutes until it becomes springy and very smooth. »

Divide the dough into two even-sized pieces and shape each into a rectangle using the length of the tin as a rough guide. Place in the prepared tins, smoothing down the tops and leave to prove (increase in size) for another 10 minutes until slightly risen.

Meanwhile, preheat the oven to 180°C (350°F), gas mark 4. Brush the tops of the loaves with the beaten egg mixture. Bake for 45 minutes until the loaves are a deep golden brown and sound hollow when tipped out of the tins and tapped on the bottom. Return to the tins and leave for 5 minutes on a heatproof surface, then transfer the bread to a wire rack and allow to cool completely before slicing.

To serve, cut the bread into slices and arrange in a bread basket with a pot of butter. Wrap any remaining bread in cling film and store in a bread bin or dark cupboard for 1–2 days.

1. Dough before being covered

2. After 1 hour: doubled in size

3. Knocking back the dough

4. Kneading with heel of hand

Multi Seed Wheaten Bread

Makes two 900g (2lb) loaves

This is the first thing we make every morning at the restaurant. Guests who have stayed overnight can wake up to the smell wafting around the house. The bread is delicious sprinkled with a couple of tablespoons of sesame seeds or sunflower seeds before baking. If you don't have any buttermilk to hand, add the juice of a lemon to the same quantity of fresh milk and leave overnight before using.

rapeseed or sunflower oil, for oiling
450g (1lb) plain flour, plus extra for dusting
450g (1lb) coarse wholemeal flour
2 tsp bicarbonate of soda
2 tsp salt
100g (4oz) wheat bran
100g (4oz) mixed seeds, such as linseed, sunflower, sesame and poppy seeds
50g (2oz) butter
2 tbsp golden syrup
2 tbsp demerara sugar
1 litre (1¾ pints) buttermilk, plus a little extra if necessary
butter, to serve

Preheat the oven to 180°C (350°F), gas mark 4 and lightly oil two 900g (2lb) loaf tins.

Sift the flours, bicarbonate of soda and salt into a large bowl. Tip the bran left in the sieve into the bowl and stir in with the wheat bran and all but 1 tablespoon of the seeds (reserve them for the top). Rub the butter in with your fingertips until evenly dispersed.

Make a well in the centre of the dry ingredients and add the golden syrup, demerara sugar and the buttermilk. Using a large spoon, mix gently and quickly until you have achieved a fairly wet dropping consistency, making sure there are no pockets of flour remaining.

Divide the mixture evenly between the prepared loaf tins, spreading it evenly and smoothing the tops with the back of a spoon. Sprinkle over the reserved tablespoon of the seeds. Bake for 1½ hours until well risen and cracked on the top and so that a skewer comes out clean when inserted in the centre.

To check the loaves are properly cooked, tip each one out of the tin and tap the base. It should sound hollow. Return to the tin and allow to cool for about 5 minutes on a heatproof surface before tipping out on to a wire rack and leaving to cool completely.

This bread is best eaten on the day it is made. To serve, place on a bread board and cut into slices at the table. Hand around with a separate pot of butter.

Mediterranean Gluten-free Bread

Makes one 900g (2lb) loaf

olive oil, for oiling

600g (1lb 6oz) gluten-free flour

½ tsp salt

2 tsp bicarbonate of soda

300g (11oz) soya bran

150g (5oz) light muscovado sugar

3 eggs

100ml (3½fl oz) Sun-dried Tomato Pesto (see page 208)

1 litre (1¾ pints) buttermilk

1 tbsp sesame seeds

butter, to serve

I've always had a tremendous response when I've served gluten-free recipes and this excellent recipe came from a pastry chef at Killybegs College, Noleen Boyle, who is coeliac herself. Don't be surprised that it has a slightly different texture to ordinary bread. It stays fresh for about 2 days, so if you want to keep it for any longer cut into slices and freeze, then place in the oven to thaw out (for 8–10 minutes at 180°C/350°F/gas mark 4) or use a toaster. Gluten-free flour is now available from all major supermarkets and health food shops or can be bought online.

Preheat the oven to 180°C (350°F), gas mark 4. Lightly oil a 900g (2lb) loaf tin.

Sift the flour into a large mixing bowl with the salt and bicarbonate of soda, then stir in the soya bran and sugar.

Place the eggs, Sun-dried Tomato Pesto and buttermilk in a jug and mix well to combine.

Make a well in centre of the dry ingredients and pour in the buttermilk mixture, mixing to combine. Spoon the mixture into the oiled loaf tin and smooth the surface, using the back of a spoon. Sprinkle the sesame seeds on top.

Bake the bread for 1 hour until golden brown and crusty on top. Tip briefly from the tin and tap the base of the loaf to check it is cooked – it should sound hollow. Return to the tin and leave for 5 minutes on a heatproof surface, then turn the bread out on to a wire rack and allow to cool completely.

Once the bread has cooled down completely, place on a bread board and cut into slices at the table. Serve with butter.

Walnut & Fig Bread

Makes 2 round loaves

550g (1lb 3½oz) strong plain white flour, plus extra for dusting

1 tsp salt

50g (2oz) butter, diced and chilled

7g sachet of easy blend dried yeast

100g (4oz) walnuts, roughly chopped

50g (2oz) dried ready-to-eat figs, finely chopped

sunflower oil, for oiling

butter, to serve

This is a delicious breakfast bread and also makes a lovely sandwich filled with creamy blue cheese and rocket. Also try with Chicken Liver Pâté with Fig Jam (see page 83) or Red Onion Marmalade (see page 209). I find that it toasts very well after a day or two.

Sift the flour and salt into a large bowl. Rub in the butter until the mixture resembles fine breadcrumbs. Stir in the yeast, walnuts and figs until evenly combined.

Make a well in the centre of the dry ingredients and then pour in 350ml (12fl oz) lukewarm water. Quickly mix to a smooth dough, then turn out on to a lightly floured work surface and knead for 10 minutes until smooth and elastic. Place in an oiled bowl, cover with oiled cling film and leave to rise in a warm place for about 1 hour or until doubled in size.

Knock the dough back by punching it lightly with a clenched fist, then divide it in half, shaping each piece into a smooth round. Put on baking sheets lined with non-stick baking paper and cover each one with a damp tea towel. Leave to rise again in a warm place for about 30 minutes.

Preheat the oven to 220°C (425°F), gas mark 7. Remove the damp tea towel from the loaves and slash the tops 4–5 times with a sharp knife. Bake for 10 minutes, then reduce the oven temperature to 190°C (375°F), gas mark 5 and bake for another 25–30 minutes, swapping the sheets on the oven shelves halfway through cooking.

When cooked, the loaves should sound hollow if tapped on the bottom. Transfer to a wire rack and allow to cool completely. The bread can be wrapped in cling film and stored in a bread bin for 1–2 days.

To serve, arrange a loaf on a bread board and cut into slices at the table. Serve with butter.

Cheddar & Spring Onion White Soda Bread

Makes one 15cm (6in) round loaf

450g (1lb) plain flour, plus extra for dusting
1 tsp bicarbonate of soda
1 tsp salt
100g (4oz) strong Cheddar, grated
4 spring onions, trimmed and finely chopped
350ml (12fl oz) buttermilk, plus a little extra if necessary

This is a delicious variation on a classic Irish recipe. Experiment with other flavourings such as finely chopped sun-dried tomatoes or crispy pieces of smoked bacon. If you don't have buttermilk, use fresh milk mixed with the juice of a lemon, and leave overnight before using.

Preheat the oven to 230°C (450°F), gas mark 8. Sift the flour, bicarbonate of soda and salt into a large mixing bowl. Make a well in the centre of the dry ingredients and stir in the Cheddar and spring onions, then add the buttermilk. Using a large spoon, mix gently and quickly until you have achieved a nice soft dough. Add a little bit more buttermilk if necessary until the dough binds together without being sloppy.

Knead the dough very lightly on a lightly floured work surface and shape into a round of roughly 15cm (6in). Place on a non-stick baking sheet and cut a deep cross in the top. Bake for 15 minutes.

Reduce the oven temperature to 200°C (400°F), gas mark 6 and bake the loaf for another 20–25 minutes or until it is evenly golden and crusty. It should sound hollow when tapped on the bottom. If it doesn't, return to the oven for another 5 minutes.

Transfer the cooked soda bread to a wire rack and allow to cool for about 20 minutes. This bread is best eaten while it is still warm, as it doesn't store well. To serve, place the soda bread on a bread board and cut into slices at the table.

Variation
Brown Soda Bread

Make as above but use 350g (12oz) plain flour mixed with 100g (4oz) coarse, stoneground wholemeal flour. Add 2 tablespoons of pinhead oatmeal to the mix before adding the buttermilk.

Red Onion, Olive & Rosemary Focaccia

Makes one 28 x 18cm (11 x 7in) loaf

This savoury Italian bread is made much like pizza. Semi sun-dried tomatoes or strips of roasted peppers also work well on top. This dough can be made even more easily in a food mixer.

7 tbsp extra-virgin olive oil, plus extra for oiling and drizzling

1 tsp easy blend dried yeast

450g (1lb) strong plain white flour, plus extra for dusting

1¼ tsp sea salt

1 large red onion, halved and cut into slices (keep them attached at the root)

100g (4oz) pitted black olives

1 sprig of rosemary, leaves stripped

salt and black pepper

Oil a 28 x 18 x 4cm (11 x 7 x 1½in) baking tin and line with non-stick baking paper. Mix the yeast, flour and ¼ teaspoon of salt in a large mixing bowl. Make a well in the centre and pour in 225ml (8fl oz) lukewarm water and 5 tablespoons of olive oil. Mix well to form a soft dough, then turn out on to a lightly floured work surface and knead for 10 minutes until smooth and elastic. Place in an oiled mixing bowl, cover with oiled cling film and leave to rise in a warm place for about 1 hour or until doubled in size.

Turn the dough out on to a lightly floured surface and knock it back, punching lightly to knock out air bubbles, then knead for another 2–3 minutes. Roll out to a large rectangle about 1cm (½in) in thickness. Place in the prepared tin. Cover with oiled cling film and leave to rise again for 30 minutes – it should look soft and pillowy.

Meanwhile, preheat the oven to 220°C (425°F), gas mark 7. Heat 1 tablespoon of the olive oil in a small roasting tin and toss in the red onion. Season with salt and pepper and spread in an even layer, then roast for 15–20 minutes until just tender but not coloured.

Prick the risen dough all over with a fork. Stud with the olives, fan out the red onions on top, then scatter with the rosemary and the rest of the salt, and drizzle with the remaining olive oil. Bake for about 30 minutes until risen, cooked through and golden brown. Don't worry that the onions will have tinged at the edges.

Leave in the tin for a few minutes, then turn out on to a wire rack to cool and drizzle with a little extra olive oil to keep the crust soft. Cut into chunks to serve. This is best served warm but also reheats well in a low oven or is fine when cold. To store, allow to cool, wrap in cling film and store in a bread bin for 1–2 days.

Tomato & Parmesan Twister Bread Rolls

Makes 24 rolls

For the dough

| 1 tbsp olive oil, plus extra for oiling |
| 350g (12oz) strong plain bread flour, plus extra for dusting |
| 1 tsp salt |
| 7g sachet of easy blend dried yeast |
| 1 egg beaten with 1 tbsp milk |

For the filling

| 200g (7oz) Tomato Sauce (see page 214) |
| 125g (4½oz) Pesto (see page 208) |
| 75g (3oz) freshly grated Parmesan cheese |

These bread rolls are easy to make and taste so much better than any you can buy in the shops. You can vary the fillings – try sun-dried tomato paste, tapenade, red onion marmalade, finely chopped sun-dried tomatoes or different cheeses – but go light on them or the fillings may burn while they are cooking. Turn the page for step-by-step pictures.

Preheat the oven to 200°C (400°F), gas mark 6. Lightly oil two 12-hole muffin tins.

Sift the flour into a large mixing bowl with the salt and stir in the dried yeast. Make a well in the centre and pour in the olive oil and 300ml (11fl oz) lukewarm water. Mix to a smooth dough.

Turn the dough out on to a lightly floured work surface and knead for 5–10 minutes, pushing and stretching the dough until smooth and elastic. Alternatively, use a food mixer with the dough hook attached and set on a low speed.

Place the dough in a large, lightly oiled bowl. Cover with a clean tea towel and leave in a warm place for 1 hour until the dough has almost doubled in size.

Knock the risen dough back, punching it lightly to knock out large air bubbles and knead it briefly on a lightly floured work surface. With a rolling pin, roll out the dough into a large rectangle, approximately 55 x 35cm (22 x 14in). Using a palette knife, spread over the tomato sauce and then spread the pesto on top. Sprinkle over the Parmesan cheese. Then, starting from one of the long edges, gently roll the dough away from you into a long Swiss roll shape. Don't worry if it sticks a little, just gently coax it up a bit at a time with floured fingers until it reaches the other side and then press the seam together to stick. »

Cut the roll into 4cm (1½in) thick slices and place in the tin, one in each muffin hole, with one of the cut sides facing down. Brush the tops lightly with the beaten egg mixture and leave them to rise in a warm place for another 10 minutes or until doubled in size.

Bake the rolls for 20–25 minutes, swapping the tins on the shelves halfway through, until cooked through and golden brown. Leave the rolls in the muffin tins for a couple of minutes and then loosen them from the tins with a knife and slide out on to a wire rack. Serve warm or allow to cool completely.

To serve, pile the rolls into a bread basket and place on the table. These are best eaten warm on the day they are made, or you can freeze in an airtight container for 1 month. To thaw, wrap in foil and bake in the oven at 180°C (350°F), gas mark 4, for 8–10 minutes.

1. Roll the dough into a rectangle

2. Spread with fillings

3. Roll up the dough

4. Cut into slices and place in tin

Canapés, Soups & Starters

Sticky Beef Skewers

Makes 20

These moreish skewers are shown in the picture on pages 58–9. For hassle-free canapés, most of the preparation can be done in advance. You can marinate the beef up to a day beforehand and store uncooked in an airtight container in the fridge. Soak the skewers in cold water for at least 30 minutes before use (this prevents them burning during cooking) and then skewer the beef up to 12 hours in advance.

2 garlic cloves, peeled and crushed
3 tbsp runny honey
I tbsp sweet chilli sauce
I tbsp Worcestershire sauce
I tbsp dark soy sauce
I tbsp balsamic vinegar
I tsp whole grain mustard
450g (1lb) sirloin steak, trimmed of any fat and cut into thin strips
Garlic and Chive Mayonnaise, to serve (see page 209)

Place the garlic in a large, shallow non-metallic dish and add the honey, sweet chilli sauce, Worcestershire sauce, soy sauce, balsamic vinegar and mustard. Mix until well combined. Thread the sirloin strips on to twenty 10cm (4in) soaked bamboo skewers and add the marinade, turning to coat. Cover with cling film and chill in the fridge for at least 6 hours, or for up to 24 hours.

Preheat the grill to medium. Drain the beef skewers, reserving any remaining marinade, and arrange on a grill rack. Cook for 5–6 minutes until cooked through and well caramelised, turning once.

Meanwhile, place the reserved marinade in a small pan and allow it to simmer over a medium heat until it is thick and syrupy and reduced by half. Stir in any cooking juices from the grill pan and then brush the sauce over the cooked beef skewers.

Arrange the sticky beef skewers on a large warmed platter around a bowl of Garlic and Chive Mayonnaise, for dipping.

Sausage Rolls
with Sesame Seeds

This is classic party food! These are ideal to prepare in advance as they can be frozen uncooked for up to one month. Layer between sheets of non-stick baking paper in a plastic rigid container and secure with a lid before freezing. Even more convenient, they can be cooked straight from frozen – simply increase the cooking time by about 10 minutes.

Makes 40

25g (1oz) butter
2 tbsp finely diced onion
3 eggs
450g (1lb) good-quality sausage meat
2 tbsp sweet chilli sauce
1 tbsp chopped fresh basil
1 tbsp double cream
500g (1lb 2oz) ready-rolled puff pastry, thawed if frozen
plain flour, for dusting
2 tbsp sesame seeds
salt and freshly ground black pepper

Preheat the oven to 220°C (425°F), gas mark 7. Melt the butter in a frying pan and sauté the onion over a medium heat for about 5 minutes until softened but not browned. Remove from the heat and allow to cool.

Break two eggs into a food processor or liquidiser and add the sausage meat, sweet chilli sauce, basil and cream. Blend for 2 minutes until smooth, then scrape out into a bowl and stir in the cooked onions. Season with salt and pepper and spoon the mixture into a piping bag fitted with a 2cm (¾in) plain nozzle. Chill in the fridge for at least 30 minutes to firm up a little.

Beat the remaining egg in a small bowl with a pinch of salt and set aside to use for glazing. Roll the puff pastry out on a lightly floured surface to a 40 x 30cm (16 x 12in) rectangle and then cut into four strips, each measuring 30 x 10cm (12 x 4in). Pipe the sausage meat mixture in a fairly thick line down the centre of each pastry strip and brush along one long edge of the pastry with a little of the beaten egg. Roll up to enclose and press down the edges firmly to seal.

Brush the four large sausage rolls with the remaining beaten egg and sprinkle lightly with the sesame seeds. Cut each roll into 2.5cm (1in) lengths, wiping the knife each time to clean off the sausage meat and arrange on two large baking sheets lined with non-stick baking paper. Bake for 15 minutes or until crisp and golden. Arrange on a warmed platter to serve.

Sesame Prawn Toasts

Makes 24

A Chinese takeaway favourite, these are shown in the picture on page 58. They are so easy to make – simply whiz the prawn mixture in a food processor before spreading on the bread. It is best to use bread that is a couple of days old, so that it has dried out slightly and is not too doughy. I like to serve these with a dipping sauce, but they are also great with just a squeeze of lime.

To make the dipping sauce, place the soy sauce in a small bowl and stir in the honey, sesame oil and sweet chilli sauce. Cover with cling film. This will keep in the fridge for up to 2 weeks.

Place the prawns in a food processor or blender with the egg white, cornflour, lemon juice, soy sauce, sweet chilli sauce, garlic, ginger and mustard. Blend to form a smooth paste. This can be made up to 24 hours in advance.

Spread the prawn paste over the bread slices (avoiding the edges as the crusts will be trimmed off later) and sprinkle the sesame seeds evenly over each slice, pressing them down gently with your fingertips. Arrange the slices of prawn-topped bread on a baking sheet or plastic tray, then cover with cling film and chill for up to 1 hour.

Preheat the vegetable oil to 180°C (350°F) in a deep-fat fryer or a large, deep-sided saucepan. Deep-fry the toasts in batches for about 1–1½ minutes on each side or until golden. Drain on kitchen paper and then cut off the crusts and cut each slice into four triangles. Cover loosely with foil, to keep warm, while the remaining toasts are being cooked.

Arrange the sesame prawn toasts on warmed plates or on one large serving platter with small bowls of the dipping sauce to serve.

For the prawn toasts

225g (8oz) peeled raw prawns, cleaned

1 egg white

1 tsp cornflour

1 tsp fresh lemon juice

1 tsp dark soy sauce

1 tsp sweet chilli sauce

1 small garlic clove, peeled and crushed

½ tsp freshly grated root ginger

1 tsp Dijon mustard

6 slices of 1–2 day-old white bread (see recipe introduction)

4 tbsp sesame seeds

vegetable oil, for deep-frying

For the dipping sauce

6 tbsp light soy sauce

2 tbsp runny honey

1 tsp toasted sesame oil

1 tbsp sweet chilli sauce

Salt Cod Fritters

Salt cod is available from fishmongers, large supermarkets and some ethnic shops and needs to be soaked in cold water before use. An hour or two should suffice if only lightly salted, or up to 24 hours if very dried out. If in doubt, check with your fishmonger or follow the packet instructions. The fritters are shown with the canapés on page 58, and are also delicious as part of a smoked fish platter.

450g (1lb) potatoes, peeled and cut into chunks
150g (5oz) salt cod, soaked (see recipe introduction)
olive oil, for cooking
1 small onion, peeled and finely chopped
2 garlic cloves, peeled and finely chopped
2 tbsp chopped flat-leaf parsley
1 egg, lightly beaten
plain flour, for dusting
Maldon sea salt and freshly ground black pepper
Aïoli, to serve (see page 209)

Cook the potatoes, covered, in a saucepan of boiling salted water for 15–20 minutes until tender. Drain well, mash until smooth and set aside.

Poach the soaked salt cod in a small pan, with just enough water to cover, for about 10 minutes, then drain and roughly flake the flesh, removing all the skin and bones. Place in a large bowl.

Meanwhile, heat 2 tablespoons of olive oil in a small frying pan over a medium heat and cook the onion and garlic for about 5 minutes until soft but not browned. Stir the cooked onion and garlic, the flaked salt cod, parsley and egg into the mashed potatoes, mix to combine and season with black pepper. Taste the mixture at this stage to see if you need to season it with salt – you may not need any depending on how salty the fish is.

With floured hands, shape the mixture into twenty small balls. Flatten the balls slightly into 5cm (2in) round patties about 1cm (½in) thick. Arrange the patties on a large flat plate and cover with cling film. Chill in the fridge for about 30 minutes to allow the mixture to firm up a little.

Heat a thin film of olive oil in a large frying pan and cook the fritters in batches for 2–3 minutes on each side until crisp and golden brown. Drain the fritters briefly on kitchen paper and cover loosely with foil to keep warm while you cook the remainder.

Serve the fritters with a bowl of Aïoli on a large, warmed platter.

Spanakopita

Makes 24

These tasty morsels remind me of holidays on the Greek islands. Look out for authentic Greek filo pastry, a far superior product to the regular filo that you get in most supermarkets.

Preheat the oven to 180°C (350°F), gas mark 4. Heat the oil in a large saucepan and add the onion, then cook gently for 2–3 minutes until softened but not browned. Add the spinach a handful at a time, stirring constantly, until it has all wilted down. Tip into a sieve and drain well, pressing out all the excess liquid with a wooden spoon. Allow to cool.

Crumble the feta cheese into a bowl and then mix in the egg, Parmesan, cooled spinach mixture, nutmeg and mint. Season with salt and pepper to taste. Melt the butter in a small pan and allow to cool a little.

Unroll the sheets of pastry and cut the stack lengthways into strips about 6cm (2½in) wide. Brush the top layer with melted butter. Place a heaped teaspoonful of the filling in the centre of one strip, at the nearest end to you, and fold one bottom corner of the top layer of pastry diagonally over the filling, so that the corner touches the opposite side to make a triangle. Then fold over the filled triangular corner, and continue folding it along the whole strip into a triangular parcel. Repeat to use all the pastry and filling – you should end up with 24 parcels in total.

Brush the underside of each spanakopita with a little of the melted butter and place on a baking sheet lined with non-stick baking paper. Brush the tops with the rest of the melted butter and bake for 15–20 minutes until crisp and golden brown. Allow to cool for a few minutes before arranging on plates or a large platter to serve.

Ingredients
1 tbsp olive oil
1 small onion, peeled and finely chopped
250g (9oz) spinach, thick stalks removed and leaves finely shredded
75g (3oz) feta cheese
1 small egg
2 tsp freshly grated Parmesan cheese
pinch of freshly grated nutmeg
2 tsp chopped mint
75g (3oz) unsalted butter
275g (10oz) filo pastry, thawed if frozen (about 6 sheets in total)
Maldon sea salt and freshly ground black pepper

Sang Choy Bow

Makes about 35

Sang Choy Bow are bite-sized pieces of food wrapped in lettuce before eating. Variations can be found in most Chinese restaurants. The secret to making them is to prepare all of the ingredients well in advance. I normally use the smaller inner crisp leaves of little gem lettuce but you could use iceberg lettuce or chicory leaves. Break the leaves into similar sizes, place in a plastic bag and keep in the fridge until you need them.

2 tbsp dry sherry

2 tsp cornflour

2 tbsp light soy sauce

4 tbsp hoisin sauce

I tsp light muscovado sugar

175ml (6fl oz) chicken stock (see page 219)

2 tbsp sunflower oil

3 garlic cloves, peeled and crushed

6 spring onions, trimmed and thinly sliced, green separated from white

450g (1lb) minced chicken

225g tin of water chestnuts, drained and finely chopped

3 tbsp chopped coriander

4 little gem lettuces, broken into individual leaves (see recipe introduction)

salt and freshly ground black pepper

Place the sherry in a small bowl and stir in the cornflour to form a smooth paste. Stir in the soy sauce, hoisin sauce, sugar and chicken stock until well combined. This sauce can be made in advance and chilled for up to 24 hours until needed.

Heat the sunflower oil in a wok or large frying pan over a medium heat. Stir-fry the garlic and the whites of the spring onions for 2–3 minutes until softened and just turning golden. Increase the heat to high, add the minced chicken and fry for about 5 minutes until just cooked through and beginning to brown, breaking up the chicken using the back of a spoon to ensure there are no big lumps. Add the water chestnuts and cook for a further 1–2 minutes.

Push the mixture to one side and then pour the prepared sauce into the wok, stirring until it boils and thickens. This will take 1–2 minutes. When the liquid is bubbling and thickened stir in the chicken mixture and mix well to combine. Season with salt and pepper to taste and stir in the green of the spring onions along with the coriander.

Arrange the lettuce leaves on a large serving platter. Spoon a small amount of the warm chicken mixture on to each lettuce leaf. Wrap up and eat with your hands.

Black Pudding Croûtes

with Red Onion Marmalade

This canapé is not as unusual as it sounds! Black pudding is often served as a tapas dish in Spain, where it is known as morcilla, and is usually homemade from a family recipe that has been passed down over many generations. Don't be tempted to make these too far in advance or the croûtes will go soggy.

Preheat the oven to 200°C (400°F), gas mark 6. Arrange the French bread slices on large baking sheets in a single layer. Brush 2 tablespoons of the oil on the bread slices and bake for 6–8 minutes until the bread is pale golden and crisp. Allow to cool slightly.

Heat the remaining olive oil in a large frying pan and cook the black pudding slices over a medium heat for 1 minute on each side until cooked through. You may need to do this in batches. Drain on kitchen paper.

Place a piece of black pudding on each croûte and top with a small spoonful of Red Onion Marmalade. Arrange on a large platter, garnish each canapé with a little parsley and serve at once.

Makes 30

1 French stick, cut on the diagonal into 30 evenly sized slices (ends discarded)

4 tbsp olive oil

450g (1lb) black pudding, cut on the diagonal into 30 evenly sized slices

100g (4oz) Red Onion Marmalade (see page 209)

flat-leaf parsley sprigs, to garnish

Parma Ham & Rocket Rolls

Makes 20

150g (5oz) ricotta cheese
2 tbsp Pesto (see page 208)
10 slices of Parma ham
50g (2oz) wild rocket, stalks removed
Maldon sea salt and freshly ground black pepper

Shown on page 59, these are very simple but look and taste quite special. They can be made an hour in advance and kept in the fridge until you are ready to eat them. When cutting the Parma ham, don't worry if each slice is not perfect, you can neaten them up as you roll them. A great alternative to Parma ham is bresaola – very thin slices of air-dried, salted beef.

Mix the ricotta with the pesto in a small bowl and season generously with salt and pepper.

Carefully cut each slice of Parma ham in half across the width and arrange on a clean work surface. Spread a heaped teaspoon of the ricotta mixture in a thin even layer over each one, then lay a few sprigs of rocket lengthways across each slice, leaving the sprig ends hanging over the edges.

Roll each one up and arrange on a serving platter. Cover loosely with cling film and place in the fridge until you are ready to serve.

Pumpkin & Haricot Bean Soup

Haricot or cannellini beans work best for this – use the freshest you can find or they can take an age to cook. As this recipe makes such a large quantity you may wish to freeze some. Allow the soup to cool and then pour into freezer bags or containers with lids (leave enough space for expansion). To thaw the soup, leave overnight at room temperature and reheat until piping hot.

Vegetarian (if vegetable stock is used)

275g (10oz) dried white haricot beans, soaked overnight in cold water

2 tbsp finely chopped sage

4 garlic cloves, peeled and finely chopped

2 fresh bay leaves

2 thyme sprigs

2kg (4½lb) pumpkin or butternut squash

3 tbsp olive oil

2 onions, peeled and finely chopped

2 carrots, peeled and finely chopped

2 celery sticks, finely chopped

3 litres (5 pints) vegetable or chicken stock (see pages 218–19)

Maldon sea salt and freshly ground black pepper

Pesto, to garnish (see page 208)

rustic crusty bread, to serve

Drain the soaked beans and place in a large saucepan with plenty of cold water. Bring to the boil and boil fast for 15 minutes.

Drain the beans and rinse thoroughly in cold running water. Return the beans to the saucepan and cover them with 5cm (2in) of fresh water. Add half the sage, half the garlic, the bay leaves and thyme sprigs to the pan and bring to the boil, reduce the heat and simmer for 1 hour or until the beans are tender, topping up with boiling water if necessary. Drain and rinse briefly, discarding the bay leaves and thyme sprigs.

Meanwhile, preheat the oven to 230°C (450°F), gas mark 8. Cut the pumpkin or squash into wedges, not more than 7.5cm (3in) thick and scoop out the seeds using a large spoon. Brush all over using 1 tablespoon of the olive oil, place them in a large roasting tin and season generously with salt and pepper. Roast on a high shelf in the oven, for about 45 minutes or until softened and caramelised, turning once.

Heat the remaining 2 tablespoons of olive oil in a large saucepan. Add the remaining sage and garlic, the onions, carrots and celery and cook for 10–15 minutes until soft but not browned, stirring occasionally. Pour in the stock and bring to the boil, then season with salt and pepper and simmer for 10–15 minutes until the vegetables are completely tender and softened. »

Allow the roasted pumpkin or squash to cool, then scoop away the flesh and discard the skin – you should have about 1kg (2lb 2oz) in total. Add to the saucepan and simmer for another 15–20 minutes until the pumpkin is tender and has started to break down. Whiz the soup to a purée with a hand-held blender or in batches in a food processor, then add the cooked beans, season with salt and pepper to taste and reheat gently.

To serve, ladle the soup into warmed bowls and top each serving with a teaspoonful of pesto. Serve hot with some crusty bread.

Carrot, Ginger & Honey Soup

Serves 6–8

I love everything about this soup – it's really simple to make, the ingredients cost very little, the flavours are gorgeous and it ends up the most fantastic vibrant orange colour.

Vegetarian

75g (3oz) unsalted butter

I onion, peeled and thinly sliced

20g (¾oz) root ginger, peeled and finely chopped

700g (1½lb) carrots, grated

I tbsp runny honey

I tsp fresh lemon juice

Maldon sea salt and freshly ground white pepper

lightly whipped cream and snipped chives, to garnish

Melt the butter in a large saucepan over a medium heat. Add the onion and ginger and cook gently for 8–10 minutes until soft but not browned, stirring occasionally. Stir in the grated carrots, honey and lemon juice and season with salt and pepper to taste.

Pour 900ml (1½ pints) boiling water into the carrot mixture and bring to the boil. Turn down the heat and simmer for 45 minutes until the mixture is slightly reduced and the carrots are tender.

Remove from the heat and blitz with a hand-held blender until smooth. Season with salt and pepper to taste and reheat gently, then ladle into warmed bowls. Drizzle a little whipped cream into each bowl and garnish down the middle with a thin line of snipped chives to serve.

Beetroot Borscht

Serves 4–6

Borscht is a classic soup in most parts of Eastern Europe and it was Piotr and Pawel, twin polish chefs, who first introduced it to my kitchen. When choosing beetroot, look for those that are plump, smooth and firm, avoiding any with signs of decay. I always grate them in a food processor to prevent my hands from staining, but if you have to do them by hand, try wearing rubber gloves!

Vegetarian (if vegetable stock is used)

I tbsp olive oil

I leek, finely chopped

I celery stick, finely chopped

275g (10oz) raw beetroot, peeled and finely grated

100g (4oz) potato, peeled and diced

150g (5oz) carrots, peeled and finely grated

1.2 litres (2 pints) vegetable or beef stock (see page 218)

2 tsp red wine vinegar

I tsp caster sugar

salt and freshly ground black pepper

soured cream and dill sprigs, to garnish

Heat the olive oil in a large saucepan over a medium heat and fry the leek and celery for about 2–3 minutes until softened but not browned, stirring occasionally. Add the beetroot, potato and grated carrot, stirring to combine.

Pour the stock into the saucepan, season with salt and pepper and bring to the boil. Reduce the heat and simmer for about 40 minutes, stirring occasionally, until the vegetables are completely tender and the soup has thickened slightly.

Season the soup with salt and pepper to taste, then stir in the vinegar and sugar. Heat gently until the sugar has dissolved. Ladle the soup into warmed bowls and garnish each with a small dollop of soured cream and dill sprigs. Serve immediately.

Chestnut & Wild Mushroom Soup

Canned chestnuts are available in larger supermarkets and good delis. Vacuum-packed chestnuts seem to be more of a seasonal product, only available around Christmas. This soup is delicious as it is, or it can be garnished with cooked, diced bacon, smoked duck or – my personal favourite – sautéed wild mushrooms and freshly baked croûtons. If you have any soup left over it freezes well – allow to cool and then pour into freezer bags or containers with lids (leave enough space for expansion). To thaw, leave the bags overnight at room temperature and reheat the soup until piping hot.

Ingredients
50g (2oz) dried mixed wild mushrooms
1 tbsp sunflower oil
450g (1lb) peeled canned or vacuum-packed chestnuts, chopped
100g (4oz) rindless smoked bacon, finely chopped
1 large onion, peeled and finely chopped
1 tsp chopped thyme leaves
1.2 litres (2 pints) chicken or vegetable stock (see page 219 or 218)
200ml (7fl oz) double cream
Maldon sea salt and freshly ground black pepper
lightly whipped cream and snipped chives, to garnish

Place the dried wild mushrooms in a heatproof bowl and pour over 400ml (14fl oz) boiling water to cover. Set aside for 20 minutes to allow the mushrooms to plump up. Drain the mushrooms, reserving the soaking liquid, and gently squeeze them dry.

Heat a large saucepan over a medium heat and add the sunflower oil. Add the chestnuts, bacon, onion and drained wild mushrooms and cook gently for 10 minutes until golden brown, stirring occasionally. Season with salt and pepper.

Add the thyme to the saucepan with the reserved mushroom soaking liquid and the stock, and stir well to combine. Bring to the boil, then reduce the heat and simmer for 20 minutes.

Stir in the double cream and allow it to heat through for 1 minute. Whiz the soup with a hand-held blender until as smooth as possible. Re-season with salt and pepper to taste and ladle into warmed wide-rimmed bowls. Garnish each one with a little drizzle of whipped cream and a sprinkling of chives or your choice of garnishes as described in the introduction. Serve at once.

Smoked Bacon & Tomato Soup

Serves 6–8

A great soup for the autumn, when there is a glut of ripe tomatoes, otherwise you can use canned ones. As no stock is added, it has a wonderfully intense tomato flavour with a slightly smoky taste. I love to serve this soup piping hot with hunks of crusty bread. It can also be served chilled on a summer's day.

2 tbsp olive oil, plus extra for drizzling
2 large onions, peeled and finely chopped
2 garlic cloves, peeled and finely chopped
350g (12oz) smoked bacon or pancetta, rind removed and meat diced
1.8kg (4lb) ripe tomatoes, roughly chopped, or 4 x 400g tins of chopped tomatoes (or use a mixture of both)
2 tbsp tomato purée
Maldon sea salt and freshly ground black pepper
Red Onion, Olive and Rosemary Focaccia, to serve (see page 45)

Heat the olive oil in a large saucepan over a high heat. Add the onions, garlic, and bacon or pancetta, and cook, stirring occasionally, for about 10 minutes or until the onions have softened and the bacon is cooked through and starting to brown.

Stir the tomatoes and tomato purée into the saucepan and season with pepper. Reduce the heat a little and cook gently, stirring occasionally, for 15–20 minutes or until the tomatoes have softened and their liquid has been released.

Blitz the soup either with a hand-held blender or in batches in a food processor until it is as smooth as possible, then pass through a fine sieve into a large, clean saucepan.

Season the soup with salt and pepper to taste, then reheat gently. To serve, ladle into warmed bowls and place the bowls on plates. Drizzle a little olive oil over each serving of soup and top each with a generous grinding of black pepper. Serve with a separate basket of the Red Onion and Rosemary Focaccia.

Velouté of Sweetcorn
with Smoked Chicken and Popcorn

A velouté is a thick, smooth, velvety soup. I like to garnish this with a sprinkling of salted popcorn, which is a bit of fun and tastes great, too! I normally use the microwaveable popcorn that is readily available in supermarkets. For a lower calorie version of the soup, simply replace the cream with milk and either halve the quantity of butter or leave it out completely.

Serves 4

1 tbsp olive oil
50g (2oz) butter
1 onion, peeled and finely chopped
1 garlic clove, peeled and crushed
275g (10oz) fresh or frozen sweetcorn kernels
250ml (9fl oz) sweet white wine, such as Riesling
1.2 litres (2 pints) chicken stock (see page 219)
300ml (11fl oz) double cream
1 tsp chopped thyme leaves
175g (6oz) smoked chicken breast, finely diced
1 tsp snipped chives or chopped chervil
Maldon sea salt and freshly ground black pepper
salted popcorn, to garnish

Heat the olive oil in a large saucepan over a medium heat and then add the butter. Once the butter is foaming, add the onion, garlic and sweetcorn. Cook for 5 minutes, stirring occasionally, until the onion mixture has softened but not browned.

Pour the white wine into the saucepan and allow to simmer for about 15 minutes until reduced by half. Stir in the chicken stock, double cream and thyme and bring to the boil. Turn down the heat and simmer for 40–45 minutes until reduced and slightly thickened, stirring occasionally.

Stir half of the diced smoked chicken into the soup and season with salt and pepper to taste. Blitz with a hand-held blender until as smooth as possible, then pass through a fine sieve into a clean, large saucepan and reheat gently. Use the hand-held blender again to blitz the soup to create a foam on top.

Divide the remaining diced smoked chicken among warmed bowls and ladle the velouté of sweetcorn on top, spooning the foam over. Sprinkle over the chives or chervil. Garnish with popcorn to serve.

Chicken, Coconut & Shiitake Mushroom Soup
with Galangal

Based on a Thai soup called Tom Kha Gai, this is a hot, spicy, sweet soup made with coconut milk. Galangal is a rhizome from the same family as ginger and has a mild peppery flavour – it can be bought in root form and used in much the same way as root ginger. While travelling around Thailand, my wife Amelda and I tasted many versions of this, including one made with seafood (Tom Kha Talay), and a vegetarian option made with tofu (Tom Kha Tofu). You may need to visit an oriental supermarket for some of the ingredients but the results are well worth the effort.

Heat the sunflower oil in a large heavy-based saucepan over a medium heat. Add the galangal, lemongrass and kaffir lime leaves and cook for 1 minute, stirring continuously.

Add the chicken strips to the saucepan with the coconut milk and stock, then stir well to combine. Bring to a simmer, then mix in the chilli sauce, Thai fish sauce and shiitake mushrooms.

Bring to a gentle boil, then reduce the heat and simmer for 6–8 minutes, stirring occasionally, until the chicken is completely tender and cooked through and all of the flavours have combined.

Season with salt and pepper to taste and stir in the lime juice. Ladle into warmed oriental-style bowls and garnish with coriander leaves.

Serves 4–6

1 tbsp sunflower oil

25g (1oz) root galangal, peeled and thinly sliced

2 lemongrass stalks, outer leaves removed and thinly sliced

4 fresh or frozen kaffir lime leaves

1 large skinless chicken breast fillet, thinly sliced

400g tin of coconut milk

500ml (18fl oz) chicken stock (see page 219)

2 tsp sweet chilli sauce

2 tsp Thai fish sauce (nam pla)

100g (4oz) shiitake mushrooms, trimmed and thinly sliced

1 tbsp fresh lime juice

salt and freshly ground black pepper

coriander leaves, to garnish

The Lobster Pot's Seafood Chowder

Serves 6–8

I onion, peeled and diced

I courgette, trimmed and diced

2 carrots, peeled and diced

300ml (11fl oz) dry white wine

900ml (1½ pints) milk

300ml (11fl oz) fish stock (see page 219)

I small onion, peeled and roughly chopped

2 whole black peppercorns

I bay leaf

75g (3oz) unsalted butter

75g (3oz) plain flour

250g (9oz) prepared fish and shellfish (see recipe introduction)

Maldon sea salt and freshly ground black pepper

chopped flat-leaf parsley, to garnish

Multi Seed Wheaten Bread, to serve (see page 40)

This classic chowder recipe has been kindly given to me by Ciaran Hearne, who runs The Lobster Pot, a popular pub near Wexford. He is the father of Sharon, the fantastic home economist who helps test all of my recipes. Ciaran uses uses 1cm (½in) cubes of skinned, fresh undyed smoked haddock, organic salmon fillet and monkfish with cooked mussel meat, cooked baby squid and cooked peeled prawns but you can, of course, experiment with your own selection. Just steer clear of smoked fish as the flavour will be overpowering. This soup can be prepared in advance on the day you plan to serve it, then cooled and chilled until needed.

Place the onion, courgette and carrots in a small saucepan with the wine, if necessary adding some water so that the vegetables are just covered with liquid. Cover the pan, bring to the boil and then reduce the heat to allow the vegetables to simmer gently for about 5 minutes or until just tender.

Meanwhile, make the béchamel base for the soup. In another small saucepan, gently heat the milk and fish stock with the chopped onion, peppercorns and bay leaf until just coming to the boil. Remove from the heat and set aside to infuse.

Melt the butter in a large saucepan, then stir in the flour to make a roux. Remove from the heat. Strain the warmed béchamel through a fine sieve into a jug. Gradually add it to the roux mixture, stirring continuously until all the liquid is added and the mixture is completely smooth. Return to a gentle heat and simmer for about 4–5 minutes, stirring constantly, until the sauce has thickened.

Add the cooked vegetables and any remaining liquid to the sauce. Gently stir in the fish and shellfish and cook gently over a low heat for 3–4 minutes until all the fish is just cooked and the shellfish is heated through. Season with salt and pepper to taste. Ladle into warmed bowls and garnish with parsley. Serve immediately with slices of the Multi Seed Wheaten Bread.

Crispy Fried Prawns in Kataifi Pastry

with Chilli Jam and Lemon Mayonnaise

Serves 4

Kataifi is a finely shredded pastry which can be bought in Asian markets or deli shops. When raw, it looks like vermicelli noodles; when cooked, like a shredded wheat breakfast cereal. It should be treated delicately like filo pastry, and keeps for up to 3 months in the fridge if in its original packaging.

150g (5oz) frozen kataifi pastry (see recipe introduction)

25g (1oz) plain flour

1 egg

50ml (2fl oz) milk

12 fresh Dublin Bay prawns, peeled and veins removed

groundnut oil, for deep-frying

Maldon sea salt and freshly ground black pepper

Chilli Jam (see page 215) and Lemon Mayonnaise (see page 209), to garnish

mixed salad leaves lightly dressed with French Vinaigrette (see page 220), to serve

Allow the pastry to thaw, still in its plastic wrapping, for a minimum of 2 hours before using. Once thawed, it will be soft and pliable and ready to use, but remember that you must always keep it well covered with a clean, damp tea towel when not in use.

Place the flour in a shallow dish and season it generously with salt and pepper. In a separate shallow dish, beat the egg with the milk and a pinch of salt.

Toss the prawns in the seasoned flour until lightly coated, then dip briefly in the beaten egg mixture. Next, wrap the prawns in the kataifi pastry: lay about 5g (¼oz) of the pastry in a rectangle on a board. Sit a prawn at the end closest to you, across the width of the pastry and then roll it up away from you to completely enclose. Place the wrapped prawns, well spaced apart, on a baking sheet lined with a piece of non-stick baking paper. Cover the prawns with cling film and chill until ready to use; they will sit happily for up to 4 hours in the fridge.

Just before serving, heat the groundnut oil in a deep-fat fryer or a deep-sided saucepan to 160°C (325°F). Cook the wrapped prawns in batches of three for about 3 minutes, turning halfway through with tongs, until crisp, golden brown and cooked through. Drain on kitchen paper.

To serve, place three prawns on each large serving plate. Spoon a little Chilli Jam and Lemon Mayonnaise alongside. Arrange a small pile of dressed salad to the side.

Salmon Sausages
with Creamed Leeks

This is a really popular dish in the restaurant – it's a little bit unusual but will certainly impress your guests. The salmon mixture can be made up to 24 hours in advance, and the sausages can be poached and then left in the cling film until ready to fry, leaving very little to do at the last minute. See over the page for step by step pictures.

To make the sausages, blitz the diced salmon to a purée in a food processor. Season with salt and pepper, then add the egg yolk and cayenne pepper. Blend again until smooth. With the motor running, slowly add the cream through the feeder tube, stopping the machine as soon as it has been incorporated. Scrape the mixture into a bowl and stir in the finely chopped prawns and snipped chives.

Place a 20 x 25cm (8 x 10in) piece of cling film on a work surface. Spoon on one-eighth of the mixture in a thick strip across the width, then fold over the long ends of the film and roll into a sausage shape about 2.5cm (1in) thick and 9cm (3½in) long, twisting the ends to seal. Repeat to make 8 sausages and refrigerate for at least 10 minutes or for up to 24 hours.

Bring a large saucepan of water to a simmer and gently poach the salmon sausages, still in the cling film, for 5 minutes until slightly firm to the touch, turning with tongs halfway through when they rise to the surface. Carefully remove the sausages and place immediately in a large bowl of iced water to cool them down, then refrigerate until needed. They can be left at this stage for up to 24 hours.

When ready to serve, heat a large, non-stick frying pan. Carefully remove the cling film from the salmon sausages. Add the olive oil and butter to the heated frying pan and gently fry the sausages for 4–5 minutes, turning, until warmed through and lightly golden brown all over. Remove and drain on kitchen paper. Keep warm loosely covered with foil or in a low oven. »

For the sausages

450g (1lb) organic salmon fillet, skinned, boned, diced and well chilled

1 egg yolk

pinch of cayenne pepper

100ml (3½fl oz) double cream, well chilled

3 raw Dublin Bay prawns, peeled, veins removed and finely chopped

2 tsp snipped chives, plus extra to garnish

1 tbsp olive oil

knob of butter

salt and freshly ground black pepper

For the creamed leeks

2 tsp olive oil

knob of butter

4 small leeks, trimmed and thinly sliced on the diagonal

175ml (6fl oz) double cream

2 tbsp chopped basil

100g (4oz) smoked salmon, diced

Meanwhile, prepare the creamed leeks. Heat a large frying pan, add the olive oil and butter and then stir in the leeks and sauté for 2–3 minutes until they are just beginning to soften but are not browned. Pour in the cream and then stir in the basil and smoked salmon, turn down the heat and simmer gently for 4–5 minutes until the liquid has almost completely gone and the leeks are very tender. Season with salt and pepper to taste.

To serve, divide the creamed leeks among warmed plates. Cut each salmon sausage on the diagonal and carefully arrange on top. Garnish with snipped chives.

1. Spoon mixture on to cling film

2. Roll up into a sausage shape

3. Twist the ends to seal

4. Repeat to make 8 sausages

Smoked Salmon & Asparagus Tarts

Serves 6

If making these tarts when asparagus is not in season, use leeks or sprinkle a tablespoon of chopped fresh tarragon into the cases for a better flavour. You can make the pastry cases up to 24 hours in advance, or the raw cases can be frozen for up to 3 weeks.

375g (13oz) Shortcrust Pastry (see page 216), plus plain flour for dusting

4 eggs, plus 2 egg yolks

100g (4oz) asparagus tips, trimmed and cut in half crossways

225ml (8fl oz) double cream

3 tbsp snipped chives

225g (8oz) smoked salmon, diced

salt and freshly ground black pepper

green salad dressed with French Vinaigrette (see page 220), to serve

Roll out the pastry as thinly as possible on a lightly floured work surface, and use it to line six loose-bottomed 10cm (4in) round, fluted tartlet tins, of 2cm (¾in) in depth. Chill in the fridge for 10 minutes to allow the pastry to rest.

Preheat the oven to 180°C (350°F), gas mark 4. Prick the pastry bases with a fork, then line each with a circle of non-stick baking paper or foil. Fill with ceramic baking beans or dried pulses, place on a baking sheet and bake for about 12–15 minutes until the cases look set.

Carefully remove the beans and the paper or foil from each cooked pastry case. Separate one of the eggs and reserve the yolk. Brush the inside of each pastry case with the unbeaten egg white to form a seal. Return the cases to the oven for another 2–3 minutes or until firm to the touch and lightly browned. Remove from the oven and decrease the temperature to 170°C (325°F), gas mark 3.

Meanwhile, bring a small saucepan of salted water to the boil and blanch the asparagus tips for 2–3 minutes until just tender. Drain the asparagus and plunge into a bowl of iced water to prevent any further cooking. Drain again and pat dry on kitchen paper.

Place the rest of the eggs and the yolks (including the reserved one) in a bowl and whisk to combine. Beat in the double cream and chives, and season well with salt and pepper. Divide the salmon equally among the pastry cases, season with pepper, then arrange the asparagus on top. Give the cream mixture a good stir and carefully pour over the top. Bake for 10–12 minutes until just set but still slightly wobbly in the middle. Allow to rest for 5 minutes, then carefully remove from the tins and serve warm or cold with salad.

Peppered Monkfish and Chinese Greens

with Ginger Soy Sauce

Serves 4

The ginger soy sauce in this recipe is perfect for fish, but also tastes fantastic with roast duck, pork or chicken. If you want to make this dish into something more substantial, simply serve on a mound of plain boiled rice.

Combine the crushed peppercorns with 1 teaspoon of salt and rub the mixture into the monkfish medallions.

To make the sauce, place the soy sauce in a small saucepan with the honey, vinegar, tomato purée, coriander seeds, grated ginger and cream. Stir until well combined and bring to the boil. Turn down the heat and cook for 5–6 minutes until reduced to a syrup consistency. Add the stock, stir to combine and then reduce for another 3–4 minutes. Season the sauce with salt and pepper to taste and then pass through a sieve into a clean saucepan.

Meanwhile, heat a frying pan over a low–medium heat and add half of the olive oil and a small knob of the butter. Add the monkfish and cook for about 2–3 minutes on each side until just cooked through and tender, increasing the temperature for the last 30 seconds to brown the sides. Leave the fish in the pan to keep warm.

Heat a wok or sauté pan until very hot. Add the remaining olive oil and butter and tip in the pak choy. Season with salt and pepper to taste and stir-fry for 3–4 minutes until wilted.

To serve, arrange the pak choy in the centre of four warmed plates. Drizzle with a little chilli sauce and spoon the ginger sauce around the edge. Place three monkfish medallions on each plate and garnish each piece with a coriander leaf.

For the fish

1 tbsp black peppercorns, roughly crushed

4 x 200g (7oz) monkfish fillets, trimmed and each cut into three medallions of approximately 4 x 4cm (1½ x 1½in) each

2 tbsp olive oil

25g (1oz) butter, at room temperature

2 pak choy, cut on the diagonal into 4cm (1½in) pieces

2 tsp sweet chilli sauce

salt and freshly ground black pepper

coriander leaves, to garnish

For the sauce

1 tbsp dark soy sauce

2 tbsp runny or set honey

1 tbsp balsamic vinegar

1 tsp tomato purée

1 tsp coriander seeds, crushed

1 tsp freshly grated root ginger

100ml (3½fl oz) double cream

100ml (3½fl oz) beef stock (see page 218)

Seared Scallops
with Sauce Vierge

Serves 4

This simple dish uses only the creamy white part of the scallops, but don't let the corals, or roe as they are also known, go to waste. In the restaurant we blend them with butter and herbs to make a flavoured butter that is delicious with any type of seafood or melted on to a roasted fish fillet. The roe butter will keep in the fridge for up to a week or for a month in the freezer in an airtight plastic container. The sauce vierge will keep up to a week in the fridge in a sealed container.

To prepare the sauce, warm the lemon oil in a small saucepan. Add the onion and roasted pepper and gently fry for 5 minutes, stirring occasionally. Pour in the balsamic vinegar and extra virgin olive oil, then add the lemon zest and caster sugar. Cook for another 2–3 minutes until bubbling and warmed through. Season with salt and pepper to taste and stir in the chopped herbs. Keep warm over a very low heat.

Meanwhile, pat the scallops dry with kitchen paper. Detach the corals and set aside to make flavoured butter, if you wish (see recipe introduction).

Heat a large frying pan until it is quite hot. Add a thin film of sunflower oil to the pan, season the scallops, then add them to the pan (do this in batches if necessary) and sear over a high heat for 1½ minutes on each side or until richly browned and crispy. Transfer the cooked scallops to a plate and add a squeeze of lemon juice, then season with salt and pepper to taste.

To serve, spoon a quarter of the sauce vierge around the edge of a small serving plate and place three scallops in the centre of the plate. Plate up the remaining sauce and scallops in the same way. Top each one with a small pile of salad leaves.

For the scallops

12 king-sized scallops, removed from shells and cleaned

sunflower oil, for cooking

juice of ½ lemon

Maldon sea salt and freshly ground black pepper

mixed salad leaves dressed with French Vinaigrette (see page 220), to serve

For the sauce vierge

1 tbsp lemon oil

1 small red onion, peeled and finely diced

1 small roasted red pepper (from a jar is fine), finely diced

1 tbsp balsamic vinegar

5 tbsp extra virgin olive oil

finely grated zest of 1 lemon

2 tsp caster sugar

2 tsp snipped chives

1 tsp chopped basil

Spicy Chicken Salad
with Avocado Salsa

Serves 4

This salad can be served simple and rustic-looking, or for a more formal occasion you can spoon the avocado salsa into 10cm (4in) chef's rings set on plates and ladle balsamic cream around each one. Arrange the spicy chicken in the middle and garnish with a small mound of dressed salad leaves. Remove the chef's rings to serve.

To make the avocado salsa, cut the avocados in half and remove the stones, then scoop out the flesh. Dice the avocado flesh and place it in a small bowl with the tomatoes, onion, garlic, coriander, lime zest and juice and olive oil. Season with salt and pepper to taste and stir well to combine. Cover with cling film and leave at room temperature for up to 30 minutes to allow the flavours to develop.

Place the bread in a food processor or blender and whiz to form fine crumbs. With the motor running, add the curry powder, chilli powder, sesame seeds and parsley and whiz until just combined. Tip into a shallow dish and season well with salt and pepper.

Place the flour on a plate. Beat the egg and milk together in a shallow dish. Toss the chicken strips into the flour until well coated, shaking off any excess, then dip into the egg mixture and finally coat in the flavoured breadcrumbs.

Heat a deep-fat fryer to 180°C (350°F) or half fill a deep-sided saucepan with the sunflower oil. Cook the breaded chicken strips in batches for 3–4 minutes or until cooked through and golden brown. Drain on kitchen paper and keep warm in a low oven or loosely covered with foil while you are cooking the remainder.

To serve, arrange a quarter of the spicy chicken strips on each warmed plate and spoon the avocado salsa to the side. Drizzle the Balsamic Cream around the edge.

For the chicken

4 slices of 1-day old white bread, crusts removed

2 tsp medium curry powder

2 tsp mild chilli powder

2 tsp sesame seeds

1 tbsp chopped flat-leaf parsley

50g (2oz) plain flour

1 egg

1 tbsp milk

2 large skinless chicken breast fillets, cut into strips lengthways

sunflower oil, for deep-frying

salt and freshly ground black pepper

4 tbsp Balsamic Cream, to serve (see page 213)

For the avocado salsa

2 avocados

2 tomatoes, deseeded and diced

2 tbsp finely chopped red onion

1 garlic clove, peeled and crushed

2 tbsp chopped coriander

finely grated zest and juice of 2 limes

2 tbsp extra virgin olive oil

Cinnamon Roast Quail

with Smoked Bacon Lentils

Serves 4

Wild quail is a protected species in Ireland, so the quail available in the shops is all farmed. These tiny birds can easily dry out when cooking, so I cover the breasts with pancetta and stuff the cavity with flavoured butter to ensure the meat stays nice and moist.

Place the quails in a shallow non-metallic dish and rub them all over with olive oil. Sprinkle a little cinnamon over each quail, rub it evenly into the flesh and cover with cling film. Chill overnight in the fridge to allow the flavours to penetrate the flesh.

Preheat the oven to 180°C (350°F), gas mark 4. Rinse the lentils under plenty of cold running water and place in a medium saucepan, cover with water and bring to the boil. Simmer for 25 minutes or until the lentils are just tender but still holding their shape. Drain well and refresh under cold running water.

Mix together the butter, rosemary and onion in a bowl and season with salt and pepper to taste. Stuff the quails' cavities with the mixture, then wrap the crown of each bird in two slices of pancetta or one slice of Parma ham. Arrange in a small roasting tin and roast for 25–30 minutes until cooked through and tender with the top crisp and golden.

Meanwhile, heat a medium saucepan over a low heat and add the cooked lentils. Add the carrot and the stock and cook for about 8–10 minutes or until the lentils absorb almost all of the stock. Add the sugar, balsamic vinegar and tomato purée, stirring well to combine. Keep warm over a low heat.

Heat a frying pan over a medium heat and sauté the smoked bacon until it is golden brown and sizzling, then stir into the lentils with the parsley and season with salt and pepper to taste.

Spoon the lentils on to four warmed plates and place the roasted quail on top. Garnish with small bunches of fresh watercress, if liked.

For the quail

4 oven-ready quail, about 175g (6oz) each

2 tbsp olive oil

good pinch of ground cinnamon

25g (1oz) butter, softened

1 tsp chopped rosemary

1 small onion, peeled and finely chopped

8 slices of pancetta or 4 slices of Parma ham

salt and freshly ground black pepper

For the lentils

100g (4oz) Puy lentils

1 tbsp finely chopped carrot

175ml (6fl oz) chicken or beef stock (see page 219 or 218)

1 tsp light muscovado sugar

1 tsp balsamic vinegar

1 tsp tomato purée

100g (4oz) smoked bacon lardons or 5 smoked streaky bacon rashers, rinds removed and finely chopped

2 tsp chopped fresh flat-leaf parsley

watercress, to garnish (optional)

Curried Chicken Spring Rolls
with Mango Salsa

Serves 4

These can be assembled and cooked 2–3 hours before needed, but no earlier or the wrappers will go soggy. If you prefer not to deep-fry them, cook in a preheated oven at 180°C (350°F), gas mark 4. Brush with the egg wash and arrange on a baking sheet lined with non-stick baking paper. Bake for 15–20 minutes until crisp and golden brown.

Preheat the oven to 180°C (350°F), gas mark 4. Place the chicken fillets in a small roasting tin and season generously, then sprinkle evenly with curry powder. Drizzle over a little olive oil and add a tablespoon of water to the tin to stop the chicken from drying out. Bake for 12–15 minutes or until cooked through and tender. Allow to cool and then dice into small cubes, about 1 cm (½in).

To make the mango salsa, place the diced mango in a bowl and stir in the olive oil, diced roasted red pepper, sweet chilli sauce, coriander and basil. Season with salt and pepper to taste. Cover with cling film and set aside at room temperature until needed.

Heat the butter and a dash of olive oil in a frying pan and toss the spring onions and cabbage until almost tender. Add the mushrooms and toss again for 2–3 minutes until they begin to wilt. Add the sweet chilli sauce, Chilli Jam and coriander and toss until evenly combined. Season with salt and pepper to taste.

Lay a spring roll wrapper on a clean work surface. It is important not to let the wrappers dry out, so keep the rest covered with a clean, damp tea towel until you need them. Beat the egg and milk in a bowl until well combined. Imagine a diagonal line across the centre of the wrapper, brush the egg wash above that line and spoon the chicken mixture on to the centre along the line. Be careful not overfill the spring rolls or they can burst during cooking. Fold the bottom corner up over the mixture, then turn the two outside corners in and roll up to meet the eggy corner to stick. Repeat to make the remaining three rolls. »

Ingredients

2 skinned chicken breast fillets, each about 175–200g (6–7oz)

1 tbsp mild curry powder

olive oil, for cooking

knob of butter

2 spring onions, trimmed and finely chopped

½ head Savoy cabbage, core removed and finely shredded (about 300g/11oz)

150g (5oz) shiitake mushrooms, trimmed and sliced

3 tbsp sweet chilli sauce

3 tbsp Chilli Jam (see page 215)

1 tbsp chopped coriander

4 x 30cm (12in) spring roll wrappers, thawed if frozen

1 egg

1 tbsp milk

sunflower oil, for deep-frying

salt and freshly ground black pepper

For the mango salsa

1 ripe mango, peeled, stoned and finely diced

1 tbsp olive oil

1 small roasted red pepper (from a jar is fine), finely diced

2 tbsp sweet chilli sauce

1 tbsp chopped coriander

1 tbsp chopped basil

Pour the sunflower oil into a deep-fat fryer or half fill a large deep-sided saucepan and heat to 180°C (350°F). Deep-fry two of the rolls for about 4–5 minutes until golden brown, turning halfway through. Drain on kitchen paper and keep warm in a low oven or loosely covered with foil while you fry the remaining rolls.

To serve, slice each spring roll into three and arrange in the centre of a plate. Spoon a little salsa alongside and serve straight away.

Chicken Liver Pâté
with Fig Jam

You can buy many types of pâté, but I love to make my own occasionally – it's that little bit more special, particularly as this recipe was passed on to me by my mum. The pâté can be prepared ahead and will keep for 3–4 days in the fridge. Here I've made it in individual ramekins (see picture overleaf) but it can also be made in a 1.2 litre (2 pint) loaf tin lined with cling film. Simply prepare as described below but increase the cooking time to 1 hour. When completely cooled, invert on to a flat plate or board, peel away the cling film and cut into slices with a warmed knife.

To make the fig jam, heat the olive oil in a large saucepan over a medium heat, then tip in the onions and cook for 10 minutes, stirring occasionally, until soft but not browned. Stir in the figs and garlic until well combined, then pour in the red wine and balsamic vinegar. Cook for about 10 minutes until thickened slightly – the alcohol will have cooked off.

Stir in the sugar and thyme, then season with salt and pepper to taste. Blend in a food processor for 1–2 minutes until smooth and then allow to cool completely. Store in an airtight sterilised jar (see page 208) in the fridge and use as required. It will keep stored like this for up to 2 months. »

Serves 8

For the pâté

400g (14oz) fresh chicken livers, well trimmed

300ml (11fl oz) milk

100g (4oz) unsalted butter, softened

3 shallots, peeled and finely chopped

1 garlic clove, peeled and crushed

1 tsp chopped thyme

1 tbsp port

5 eggs

1 tbsp double cream

Maldon sea salt and freshly ground black pepper

For the fig jam

3 tbsp olive oil

3 red onions, peeled and sliced

225g (8oz) dried figs, chopped

1 garlic clove, peeled and crushed

150ml (¼ pint) red wine

2 tbsp balsamic vinegar

1 tsp caster sugar

1 tsp chopped thyme

thyme sprigs, Port and Balsamic Syrup (see page 214) and crusty bread, to serve

To make the pâté, place the chicken livers in a non-metallic bowl, pour the milk over them and cover the bowl with cling film. Leave in the fridge overnight. This will remove any traces of blood.

The next day, drain off the milk and pat the livers dry with kitchen paper. Melt 25g (1oz) of the butter in a sauté pan and gently sweat the shallots, garlic and thyme for 4–5 minutes until softened but not browned. Add the port and cook for another minute until evaporated. Remove from the heat and allow to cool completely.

Preheat the oven to 180°C (350°F), gas mark 4. Place the drained chicken livers in a food processor and blend for about 2–3 minutes until very smooth. Add the shallot mixture, the eggs, the remaining butter and the cream, along with plenty of salt and pepper. Blend again for about 30 seconds until well combined.

Pass the chicken liver mixture through a fine sieve into a large jug and then pour it into eight 100ml (3½fl oz) individual ramekins – the mixture should come two-thirds of the way up the sides but it will rise higher during cooking. Cover each ramekin with foil and place them in a 'bain marie' (a roasting tin half filled with boiling water). Cook for 20–25 minutes until set but still with a slight wobble in the middle. Remove from the bain marie and remove the foil, then allow to cool completely. Place in the fridge until needed.

Serve the pâté straight from the ramekins, with crusty bread and a dollop of fig jam. Garnish with thyme sprigs and, if you wish, drizzle with a little Port and Balsamic Syrup.

Miniature Venison Pies

Makes 12

Best eaten when freshly baked, these pies can also be made with other types of game, such as rabbit, hare, wild duck or pheasant. You might need to adjust the simmering time for different fillings – refer to the instructions on the meat packet or check with your butcher.

Heat the sunflower oil in a large non-stick frying pan and cook the bacon for 3–4 minutes until crisp and golden brown. Remove with a slotted spoon and set aside.

Place the flour in a shallow dish, season generously with salt and pepper, then use to dust the venison until well coated, shaking off any excess. Add the venison to the frying pan, along with the onion, and sauté for 6–8 minutes on a medium heat, stirring occasionally, until well browned.

Add the sage to the pan, stir in the stock and bring to the boil. Turn down the heat and simmer for about 40 minutes, stirring occasionally until the venison is tender and the sauce has reduced and thickened. Add a squeeze of lemon juice and stir in the cooked bacon. Season with salt and pepper to taste and allow to cool.

Meanwhile, butter a 12-hole muffin tin. Roll out three-quarters of the pastry on a lightly floured work surface and cut out twelve 13cm (5in) discs. Line the greased tin with the pastry circles, allowing any excess to hang over the edges. Roll out the remaining pastry and cut twelve 7.5cm (3in) discs for the lids. Arrange on a large baking sheet lined with non-stick baking paper. Cover the baking sheet and tin with cling film and chill for at least 30 minutes until needed.

When ready to cook, preheat the oven to 200°C (400°F), gas mark 6. Divide the venison and bacon mixture among the pastry cases, then brush inside the edges with a little water and lay the lids on top. Fold the edges of the pastry over and press together to seal. Cut a small slit with the point of a sharp knife on top of each pie. »

2 tsp sunflower oil
100g (4oz) rindless smoked streaky bacon, cut into small strips
2 tbsp plain flour, plus extra for dusting
700g (1½lb) stewing venison, well-trimmed and cut into 2cm (¾in) cubes
1 large onion, peeled and finely chopped
2 tsp chopped sage
900ml (1½ pints) chicken stock (see page 219)
squeeze of lemon juice
butter, for greasing
2 x 375g (13oz) batches of Shortcrust Pastry (see page 216)
1 egg yolk
salt and freshly ground black pepper

Mix the egg yolk in a small bowl with a pinch of salt and brush over the pies. Bake the pies for 25–30 minutes or until the pastry is crisp and well glazed.

Allow the pies to cool in the tin for a few minutes before removing. Either serve warm or allow to cool on a wire rack, then wrap individually in greaseproof paper and then with cling film. The pies will keep for up to 24 hours in the fridge.

Lamb Samosas
with Cucumber Raita

Serves 6

The filo pastry used to wrap these is surprisingly easy to work with, but do keep it covered with a clean, damp tea towel while not in use, or it may dry out. Allow the samosas to cool slightly before serving as the pastry is brittle initially and needs to soften. If you prefer to bake them, preheat the oven to 180°C (350°F), gas mark 4, arrange on a baking sheet lined with non-stick baking paper, brush with egg wash and bake for 15–20 minutes until crisp and golden brown.

Heat 2 tablespoons of the sunflower oil in a large frying pan over a medium heat. Add the onion and sauté for 2–3 minutes until softened but not browned. Add the minced lamb and brown thoroughly for 6–8 minutes, breaking up any lumps with the back of a wooden spoon.

Add the cumin seeds to the pan with the garlic, chilli, ginger, turmeric, ground coriander and garam masala. Mix well to combine and cook for another minute, stirring. Fold in the fresh coriander and season with salt and pepper to taste. Remove from the heat and set aside to cool completely.

To make the raita, place the yoghurt in a bowl with the mint, cucumber and lemon juice. Mix well to combine and season with salt and pepper to taste. Cover with cling film and chill until needed. »

For the samosas

sunflower oil, for cooking

I onion, peeled and finely chopped

450g (1lb) lean minced lamb

½ tsp cumin seeds

I garlic clove, peeled and crushed

I small red chilli, deseeded and finely chopped

I tbsp freshly grated root ginger

½ tsp each of turmeric, ground coriander and garam masala

2 tbsp chopped coriander

275g packet filo pastry, thawed (about 6 sheets in total)

I egg

I tbsp milk

salt and freshly ground black pepper

mango chutney, to serve

coriander leaves, to garnish

For the raita

200g (7oz) Greek yoghurt

2 tbsp chopped mint

100g (4oz) cucumber, deseeded and diced

2 tsp fresh lemon juice

Unroll the sheets of pastry and cut the stack lengthways into four long stacks of strips about 5cm (2in) wide. Place a tablespoonful of the filling on one strip, about 2.5cm (1in) from the end. Fold the bottom corner of the pastry diagonally over the filling, so that the corner touches the opposite side to make a triangle. Beat the egg and milk together and brush a little on the opposite end. Then fold over the filled triangular corner and continue folding it along the whole strip into a neat triangular parcel. Repeat to make the rest of the samosas – you should end up with 24 in total.

Pour some sunflower oil into a deep-fat fryer or half fill a deep-sided saucepan and heat it to 190°C (375°F). Carefully place the lamb samosas into the oil in batches and cook for 2–3 minutes until crisp and golden brown, turning with tongs halfway through cooking. Remove with a slotted spoon and drain well on kitchen paper.

Allow the samosas to cool slightly and then arrange them on plates in overlapping lines. Place a spoonful of the raita and mango chutney on each plate. Scatter the coriander over the samosas to garnish.

Crispy Bacon Salad
with Black Pudding and Poached Egg

This lovely, light salad is packed full of flavour. Don't be tempted to overcook the black pudding – it needs no more than a minute on each side. The egg on top is also delicious fried.

4 tbsp extra virgin olive oil
175g (6oz) black pudding, skinned and cut into 1cm (½in) slices
4 rashers of dry-cured bacon, rind removed
1 tsp wholegrain mustard
½ tsp runny honey
2 tbsp white wine vinegar
4 eggs (as fresh as possible)
175g (6oz) mixed baby salad leaves
salt and freshly ground black pepper
crusty bread, to serve

Heat a frying pan over a medium heat and add 1 tablespoon of the olive oil. Add the black pudding and cook for 1 minute on each side until tender. Transfer to a plate lined with kitchen paper and cover loosely with foil to keep warm.

Snip the bacon into thin strips into the frying pan, then increase the heat a little and sauté for 3–4 minutes until sizzling and lightly golden, tossing occasionally. Remove with a slotted spoon and drain on kitchen paper.

Pour 2 teaspoons of the vinegar into the pan, being careful of any spitting fat, then turn up the heat and scrape the sediment in the pan with a wooden spoon to deglaze for about 30 seconds until almost all the vinegar has been boiled off. Stir the mustard into the reduced down vinegar along with the honey and then pour everything into a small bowl. Whisk in the remaining olive oil until incorporated. Season with salt and pepper to taste.

To poach the eggs, bring a large saucepan of water to the boil. Add the remaining vinegar to the water, season with salt and reduce to a very gentle simmer. Carefully break the eggs into the water and simmer for 3–4 minutes until just cooked but still soft on the inside. Carefully remove the eggs from the pan with a slotted spoon and drain well on kitchen paper, trimming away any ragged edges of white.

Meanwhile, place the salad leaves in a large bowl. Break the black pudding into pieces, scatter them over the salad with the bacon, then drizzle with the dressing. Toss lightly to combine and arrange on four plates. Top each plate with a poached egg and some freshly ground black pepper. Serve with crusty bread.

Seared Beef Carpaccio

with Roasted Beetroot and Parmesan Shavings

Serves 6–8

Carpaccio is typically raw, but this one's a little different. Slice the beef as thinly as you can, but don't worry if it is not too perfect – a bit of rough texture gives plenty of character to the finished plates.

Preheat the oven to 220°C (425°F), gas mark 7. Remove the beef from the fridge 30 minutes before you intend to use it to allow it to come back to room temperature.

Scrub the beetroot, trim away the tops and pat dry with kitchen paper. Place in a roasting tin, drizzle with olive oil and balsamic vinegar, then season with salt and pepper. Cover with foil and roast for 40–45 minutes until easy to pierce with a knife. Allow to cool, then cut into quarters and toss in the cooking juices.

Heat a large griddle pan until smoking hot. Crush the coriander seeds using a pestle and mortar and sprinkle on to a board with the rosemary and ¼ teaspoon each of salt and pepper. Roll the beef in the mixture, pressing it down well to coat thoroughly. Place the beef in the heated pan and sear for about 6 minutes over a medium heat until well browned and slightly crisp all over, turning regularly. Remove from the heat and allow to rest on a board, uncovered, for at least 10 minutes.

Meanwhile, make the horseradish dressing. Place the horseradish and crème fraîche in a bowl with a teaspoon of water and mix well to combine, then season with salt and pepper to taste.

When the beef has rested, slice it as thinly as you can and arrange in an overlapping layer on large plates. Place the roasted beetroot alongside and drizzle some of the beetroot cooking juices on top, then drizzle over the horseradish dressing. Dress the watercress with olive oil and enough lemon juice to taste, then scatter it over the beef and beetroot. Garnish with the Parmesan shavings and add a good grinding of black pepper to serve.

Ingredients
450g (1lb) beef fillet (preferably well hung), completely trimmed of fat and sinew, approximately 5–7.5cm (2–3in) wide and 7.5cm (3in) long
700g (1½lb) baby beetroots
2 tbsp olive oil, plus extra for dressing
4 tbsp balsamic vinegar
2 tsp coriander seeds
1 tbsp finely chopped rosemary
2 tbsp freshly grated horseradish
100g (4oz) crème fraîche
75g (3oz) watercress, well picked over
½ lemon, pips removed
Maldon sea salt and freshly ground black pepper
50g (2oz) Parmesan cheese shavings, to garnish

Spicy Goat's Cheese
with Polenta, Chilli Jam and Pesto

This goat's cheese is coated in spicy crumbs, then deep-fried and served on golden squares of polenta. The polenta can be prepared up to 2 days in advance and kept covered with cling film in the fridge. They can also be enjoyed separately – try covering them with Tomato Sauce (see page 214), a little mozzarella and a sprinkling of Parmesan, then bake in the oven at 200°C (400°F), gas mark 6, for 20–25 minutes until bubbling and golden.

Mix the breadcrumbs in a shallow dish with the curry powder, chilli powder, turmeric, sesame seeds and parsley. Beat the egg in a separate shallow bowl. Dip each slice of goat's cheese into the beaten egg and then into the breadcrumb mixture so that it is completely coated. Arrange on a flat plate lined with non-stick baking paper and chill for at least 1 hour, or overnight, to allow the breadcrumbs to set.

Meanwhile, pour the stock into a saucepan and bring to the boil. Add the diced pepper, chilli sauce, pesto and Parmesan. Pour in the polenta, stirring all the time. Cook for 4–5 minutes until the mixture starts to come away from the sides of the pan. Pour the polenta into an 18cm (7in) square baking tin lined with non-stick baking paper. Allow to cool and then cover and chill for at least 30 minutes until firm.

When ready to serve, preheat the oven to 180°C (350°F), gas mark 4. Heat the sunflower oil in a deep-fat fryer or a deep-sided saucepan to 180°C (350°F). To check the temperature, drop a basil or parsley leaf into the oil – when hot enough, the leaf should crackle. Carefully lower in the coated goat's cheese pieces, cook for 3 minutes until crisp and golden brown, then drain well on kitchen paper. Arrange on a baking sheet lined with non-stick baking paper and bake for 3–4 minutes. »

Serves 4

Vegetarian

50g (2oz) fresh white breadcrumbs

2 tsp mild curry powder

I tsp mild chilli powder

I tsp turmeric

2 tsp sesame seeds

2 tsp chopped flat-leaf parsley

I egg

4 x 4cm (1½in) thick slices goat's cheese (from a log with about 7.5cm/3in diameter)

300ml (½ pint) vegetable stock (see page 218)

I small red pepper, cored, deseeded and finely diced

I tbsp sweet chilli sauce

I tbsp Pesto (see page 208), plus extra to serve

I tbsp freshly grated Parmesan

100g (4oz) instant polenta (cornmeal/maizemeal)

sunflower oil, for deep-frying

baby mixed salad leaves dressed with French Vinaigrette (see page 220), to serve

Chilli Jam, to serve (see page 215)

Meanwhile, take the polenta from the fridge, cut into quarters and remove from the tin. Heat a large frying pan and add the olive oil. Gently fry the polenta squares for 1–2 minutes on each side until heated through and lightly golden. These can then be kept warm in the oven for 5–10 minutes if necessary.

Arrange the polenta on four warmed plates, place the goat's cheese on top and arrange a small mound of the dressed baby salad leaves on the cheese. Drizzle the Chilli Jam and pesto around the edge.

Caramelised Onion & Dolcelatte Bruschetta

with Baby Spinach Salad

Serves 4

Vegetarian

For the bruschetta

½ French stick, thinly sliced on the diagonal into 12 equal pieces (discard the end)

2 tbsp olive oil

75g (3oz) Fig Jam or Red Onion Marmalade (see page 83 or 209)

125g (4½oz) dolcelatte, Gorgonzola or Roquefort cheese, thinly sliced

salt and freshly ground black pepper

For the baby spinach salad

100g (4oz) baby spinach leaves

2 tbsp Balsamic and Honey Dressing (see page 220)

25g (1oz) Parmesan cheese, in large shavings

Bruschetta always looks really impressive as a starter and this version even more so, with the baby spinach salad on the side. Don't be tempted to make too far in advance, as the bread will go soggy. These are also perfect as nibbles to accompany drinks.

Preheat the oven to 200°C (400°F), gas mark 6. Arrange the French bread slices in a single layer on a couple of large baking sheets. Drizzle with olive oil and bake for 6–8 minutes until the bread is pale golden and crisp. Allow to cool slightly.

Spread the fig jam or red onion marmalade over the bruschetta and arrange the cheese slices on top. Season the bruschetta with pepper and place on a baking sheet. Return to the oven for another 2 minutes or until the cheese has just melted.

Meanwhile, put the baby spinach leaves in a bowl and season to taste, then add enough dressing to barely coat the leaves.

Arrange the bruschetta on plates and grind a little black pepper over the top. Place a small mound of the baby spinach salad to the side. Scatter the Parmesan shavings over the salad and serve at once.

Courgette & Parmesan Rostis
with Tomato Dressing

Serves 6

Vegetarian

550g (1lb 3½oz) courgettes, trimmed and coarsely grated
100g (4oz) ground rice
3 tbsp shredded basil leaves, plus extra sprigs to serve
75g (3oz) Parmesan cheese, freshly grated
1 egg, lightly beaten
50g (2oz) pine nuts, lightly toasted
100ml (4fl oz) olive oil
1 ripe plum tomato, deseeded and finely diced
4 sun-dried tomatoes (preserved in oil), drained and finely chopped
1 small shallot, peeled and finely chopped
100g (4oz) wild rocket
salt and freshly ground black pepper

Courgettes have a naturally high water content, so in this recipe it is important that they are squeezed dry after grating. This will ensure that the rostis are lovely and crisp, as they should be.

Squeeze the grated courgette in a clean tea towel until it is as dry as possible and tip it into a large bowl. Mix in the ground rice, basil, Parmesan, egg and pine nuts and stir thoroughly to combine. Season with salt and pepper to taste and divide into 18 evenly sized balls, then flatten slightly into patties.

Heat 1 tablespoon of olive oil in a large, non-stick frying pan over a medium heat and carefully add half of the patties. Cook for 2–3 minutes on each side or until cooked through, crisp and golden. Drain on kitchen paper and keep warm, covered loosely with foil or in a low oven. Repeat with another tablespoon of olive oil and the remaining patties.

To make the dressing, place the remaining olive oil in a bowl and add the diced plum tomato, chopped sun-dried tomatoes and shallot and then season with salt and pepper to taste. Stir until well combined.

Place a few rocket leaves down one side of four serving plates, arrange three rostis in the centre of each plate and spoon a little of the tomato dressing next to the rostis to serve.

Roasted Vegetable, Chickpea & Feta Salad

with Cumin & Lemon Dressing

When roasting the vegetables for this salad, don't overcrowd the roasting tin – it should be large enough so that the vegetables can be spread out in a thin layer. Ensure that you turn them every now and then during roasting so that they brown evenly.

Preheat the oven to 220°C (425°F), gas mark 7. Cut the butternut squash, red pepper, courgette and fennel into small, chunky, evenly sized pieces and put in a large roasting tin with the red onion and olive oil. Season with salt and pepper and toss together until evenly combined, then spread out in a single layer and roast for 20 minutes.

Meanwhile, cut the asparagus stalks in half crossways. To make the cumin and lemon dressing, heat a dry frying pan over a high heat, add the cumin seeds and shake them around for a few seconds until lightly toasted. Grind the toasted seeds into a powder using a pestle and mortar. Tip the cumin powder into a bowl, add the lemon juice and gradually whisk in the extra virgin olive oil. Season with salt and pepper to taste and set aside.

Add the asparagus to the roasting tin, turn everything over a few times and roast for another 20 minutes until all of the vegetables are just tender and slightly caramelised around the edges.

Shortly before the roasted vegetables are ready, drop the chickpeas into a small pan of boiling salted water and simmer for 3 minutes until heated through. Drain well.

Remove the vegetables from the oven. Quickly whisk the dressing again then stir it into the roasted vegetables along with the chickpeas. Season with salt and pepper to taste. Allow to cool a little, then divide among four plates and crumble the feta cheese over the top. Scatter the rocket leaves on top and serve with the Red Onion, Olive and Rosemary Focaccia.

Vegetarian

For the salad

I small butternut squash, peeled, halved and deseeded

I red pepper, cored and deseeded

I courgette, trimmed

I fennel bulb, first outer layer removed

I red onion, peeled and cut into thin wedges through the root

3 tbsp olive oil

I bunch of asparagus, trimmed

400g tin of chickpeas, rinsed and drained

175g (6oz) feta cheese

25g (1oz) wild rocket

Maldon sea salt and freshly ground black pepper

Red Onion, Olive and Rosemary Focaccia, to serve (see page 45)

For the dressing

I tsp cumin seeds

I tbsp fresh lemon juice

3 tbsp extra virgin olive oil

Baked Figs
with Parma Ham

Serves 4

12 fresh figs
10 slices of Parma ham, about 150g (5oz) in total
100g (4oz) dolcelatte or Gorgonzola cheese, rind removed and cut into small cubes
2 tbsp olive oil
40g (1½oz) wild rocket
freshly ground black pepper
Port and Balsamic Syrup, to serve (see page 214)

At certain times of year you should have no problem getting hold of nice figs for this recipe. I love to serve figs along with savoury ingredients such as this Parma ham. Another gorgeous idea is to cover slices of bruschetta with salty goat's cheese and a few chopped walnuts, then top with some ripe fig halves and drizzle with good-quality runny honey – delicious!

Preheat the oven to 200°C (400°F), gas mark 6.

Carefully trim the stalk off each fig and cut a thin slice off the base so that they sit without rocking. Using a small, sharp knife, make a cut through each fig, starting from the stalk end and cutting down about halfway. Turn each fig a quarter turn and make a second cut at right angles to the first, again cutting only halfway down. Gently open the figs out so that they resemble lotus flowers and place on a baking sheet lined with non-stick baking paper.

Remove the thin layer of fat from each slice of Parma ham and set the fat aside. Cut the Parma ham slices into narrow strips. Gently stuff scrunched up pieces of ham into the centre of each fig and top with cubes of the dolcelatte or Gorgonzola.

Press each fig together to enclose its filling. Carefully wrap the fat from the Parma ham around the figs and arrange back on the lined baking sheet. Drizzle a little olive oil over each one and season with pepper. The figs can be prepared to this stage a few hours in advance and kept covered loosely with cling film in the fridge until needed.

Bake the figs for 8–10 minutes or until the Parma ham has crisped and the cheese has melted. The figs should have softened but still retain their shape.

To serve, arrange a small mound of wild rocket on plates and arrange three figs on each one. Drizzle the Port and Balsamic Syrup around the edge of the plates to serve.

Ratatouille Puff Pizza Tart

Serves 4

These fantastic Mediterranean-style tarts look stunning served with a drizzle of basil oil. To make your own basil oil, simply place a bunch of basil in a blender with 150ml (¼ pint) of olive oil and blend until smooth. Pass through a fine sieve set over a jug and then transfer to a plastic squeezy bottle or a sterilised screw-topped jar (see page 208). Store in the fridge for up to a month.

Roll out the pastry on a lightly floured board to a 33cm (13in) square, of 5mm (¼in) in thickness. Cut out four 15cm (6in) circles from the pastry or stamp out using a fluted cutter. Place on baking sheets lined with non-stick baking paper, then chill for 30 minutes.

Meanwhile, preheat the oven to 190°C (375°F), gas mark 5 and preheat the grill to high. Rub the whole peppers with 1 tablespoon of olive oil and roast under the grill for about 20 minutes until the skins are blackened and blistered, turning regularly. Transfer to a bowl and cover with cling film, then allow to cool. Once cool, peel, deseed and cut the peppers into 0.5cm (¼in) dice.

Remove the chilled pastry from the fridge. Find a bowl or plate about 2.5cm (1in) smaller in diameter than the pastry circles. Place it on the pastry and mark around the edge to create a rim about 1cm (½in) wide. This will form a little crust.

Brush the pastry crust with a little beaten egg, being careful not to let it run down the outer edge as this will prevent the pastry from rising. Reserve the remaining beaten egg. Prick the inner circle of pastry all over with a fork (to prevent the middle from puffing up and to make a slight dip for the topping). Bake for 10–15 minutes until the edges are puffed up and lightly golden, swapping the baking sheets around in the oven halfway through to ensure the tarts cook evenly. If the inner pastry puffs up during cooking simply it push down with the back of a spoon to flatten completely. »

Vegetarian

500g packet all-butter puff pastry, thawed

plain flour for dusting

1 small red pepper

1 small yellow pepper

3 tbsp olive oil

beaten egg, for glazing

1 small courgette, trimmed and cut into 2cm (¾in) dice

1 small red onion, peeled and cut into 2cm (¾in) dice

100g (4oz) aubergine, cut into 2cm (¾in) dice

1 egg yolk, lightly beaten

4 tbsp double cream

4 tbsp freshly grated Parmesan cheese

2 tsp Port and Balsamic Syrup (see page 214)

Maldon sea salt and freshly ground black pepper

To garnish (optional)

toasted pine nuts

finely grated Parmesan cheese

wild rocket leaves

basil oil (see recipe introduction)

While the pastry is baking, heat the remaining olive oil in a frying pan over a medium heat and sauté the courgette, red onion and aubergine for 8–10 minutes until they are beginning to soften and brown. Season with salt and pepper to taste and stir in the diced roasted peppers.

Place the egg yolk in a bowl with the double cream and the reserved beaten egg. Lightly beat to combine, then stir in the cooked vegetables. Divide the vegetable mixture evenly among the pastry cases and scatter the Parmesan over the top. Return to the oven for 10–12 minutes until the vegetable mixture is just set, again swapping the baking sheets halfway through.

Arrange the cooked tarts on warmed plates, then scatter with toasted pine nuts, if you wish, and sprinkle with grated Parmesan cheese. Pile the rocket in the centre of the tarts, if using, and dress with the Port and Balsamic Syrup. Drizzle a little of the basil oil around the plates to serve.

Main Courses

Fillet of Monkfish wrapped in Parma Ham

with Potato, Leek & Pea Purée

Ask your fishmonger to give you the monkfish well trimmed, as the membrane is quite tricky to remove. The fish can be prepared ahead of time, then cooked just before serving. Also make the purée in advance and reheat at the last minute while finishing off the sauce.

Cut a slit in the side of each monkfish piece to create a pocket. Push the peppers and two-thirds of the basil inside, then season with salt and pepper. Close the pockets, sandwiching in the mixture. Lay two Parma ham slices on the work surface, slightly overlapping, then place a monkfish fillet on top and wrap up. If it won't stay together properly, tie with butcher's string at 2.5cm (1in) intervals. Repeat with the remaining fillets. Set aside while you cook the vegetable purée.

To make the purée, heat 25g (1oz) of the butter along with the olive oil in a large, heavy-based saucepan. Add the leek, cover and cook gently for 10–15 minutes until soft but not browned, stirring occasionally. Add the potatoes and stock to the pan, then bring to the boil. Reduce the heat and simmer for 10–15 minutes. Add the peas, cover and simmer for 8 minutes until everything is tender.

Strain the vegetables, reserving the cooking liquid. Place the liquid in a small pan and simmer until reduced to 100ml (4fl oz). Place the cooked vegetables in a food processor with the cream and blitz to make a purée. Season with salt and pepper, return to a clean pan and keep warm over a low heat.

To cook the fish, preheat the oven to 190°C (375°F), gas mark 5 and heat the olive oil in a large ovenproof frying pan. Sear the wrapped monkfish pieces in the pan on all sides for 3–4 minutes until the ham is crisp and golden. Transfer to the oven and roast for 8–10 minutes until firm to the touch and just cooked through.

Remove the monkfish from the oven and transfer to a carving board. Cover the fish loosely with foil and allow it to rest. **»**

For the monkfish

4 x 175g (6oz) monkfish tail fillets

50g (2oz) roasted red peppers (from a jar is fine), thinly sliced

4 tbsp shredded basil

8 thin slices of Parma ham, about 175g (6oz) in total

1 tbsp extra virgin olive oil

salt and freshly ground black pepper

For the purée

40g (1½oz) unsalted butter

1 tbsp extra virgin olive oil

1 leek, trimmed and thinly sliced, about 225g (8oz) in total

175g (6oz) potatoes, peeled and cubed

300ml (11fl oz) chicken stock (see page 219)

175g (6oz) shelled peas

3 tbsp double cream

juice of ½ lemon

Strain any juices released from the fish, through a sieve, into the reduced vegetable cooking liquid, then squeeze in enough lemon juice to taste. Bring to the boil, then boil fast for 4 minutes. Remove from the heat, add the remaining shredded basil and unsalted butter, and whisk to combine. Season with salt and pepper.

Slice each fish parcel into four (remove the string if used). Divide the vegetable purée among plates and arrange the monkfish slices on top, then spoon the sauce around the edge to serve.

Spaghetti & Clams
with Chilli and Parsley

Serves 4

In Naples, this meal is known as the Feast of the Seven Fishes and is served on Christmas Eve. The Italians traditionally leave the table still hungry for the Christ Child, but I'm sure your guests won't be hungry after eating this delicious dish. Look out for amande, palourd or carpet shell clams as they have the best flavour, and make sure they're really fresh before buying them.

350g (12oz) dried spaghetti
1.8kg (4lb) small clams
150ml (¼ pint) extra virgin olive oil
2 garlic cloves, peeled and finely chopped
good pinch of dried chilli flakes
1 tbsp chopped flat-leaf parsley
Maldon sea salt and freshly ground black pepper

Cook the spaghetti in a large saucepan of boiling salted water according to the packet instructions. Wash the clams thoroughly in a bowl under cold running water to get rid of all of the sand in the shells. Discard any that do not close when sharply tapped.

Meanwhile, heat the olive oil in a large frying pan with a lid over a medium heat and sauté the garlic for 10–20 seconds until sizzling. Add the clams, give the pan a good shake and cover with the lid. Cook for a couple of minutes over a medium heat until the shells open, then immediately remove from the heat.

Remove the clams from the pan with a slotted spoon, discarding any that have not opened. Reserve about half of the clams and remove the remainder from their shells. Return all of the clams to the cooking liquid in the pan and add the chilli flakes and parsley.

Drain the spaghetti in a colander and then tip it into the clam mixture. Stir over a gentle heat for a minute or two so that the pasta absorbs the broth and flavour of the clams. Divide among warmed pasta bowls and serve at once.

Herb-crusted Turbot

with Potato Purée and Chive Velouté

Serves 4

This is a very popular MacNean dish. Ask your fishmonger for the trimmings from the turbot, or if trimming the fish yourself, retain the skirt (the frilly part around the edges), to use in the sauce. If turbot is not available, use brill or halibut instead.

Place the breadcrumbs and herbs in a food processor and blend until the crumbs are green and fragrant. Season the turbot on both sides with salt and pepper and arrange on a baking sheet lined with non-stick baking paper. Brush the fillets with the egg yolk, then sprinkle the breadcrumbs in a thin, even layer. Place in the fridge for at least 10 minutes to allow the crust to set, loosely covered with cling film. Cook within 4 hours.

To make the velouté, melt the butter in a saucepan over a medium heat. Add the shallot and leek and cook for 2–3 minutes until soft but not browned. Add the fish trimmings and cook for another 2–3 minutes, stirring. Pour in the Noilly Prat or Martini and simmer for about 5 minutes until almost all the liquid has gone. Pour in the stock and cook for about 3 minutes until reduced by half, then stir in the cream.

Bring to the boil, reduce the heat and simmer for another 3–4 minutes until the sauce has slightly reduced and thickened. Season with salt and add cayenne pepper to taste. Strain through a fine sieve into a bowl and discard the fish trimmings. This can now be left to cool. Keep in the fridge, covered with cling film, until needed.

When you are ready to cook, preheat the oven to 180°C (350°F), gas mark 4. Place the potatoes in a large saucepan and cover with cold water, then bring to the boil. Add a pinch of salt, reduce the heat and simmer for 20–25 minutes or until the potatoes are tender. Drain well and mash until smooth. Heat the cream, milk and butter together in a small pan. Gradually beat into the mashed potatoes and season with salt and pepper to taste. Keep warm. »

For the turbot

50g (2oz) fresh white breadcrumbs

15g (½oz) mixed herbs (e.g. basil, flat-leaf parsley and tarragon)

4 x 175g (6oz) turbot fillets, trimmed and skinned

1 egg yolk, beaten

15g (½oz) butter

4 small vines of cherry tomatoes

Maldon sea salt and freshly ground black pepper

For the chive velouté

40g (1½oz) butter

1 shallot, peeled and finely chopped

1 tbsp finely chopped leek

50g (2oz) white fish trimmings (from turbot is perfect)

100ml (4fl oz) Noilly Prat or dry Martini

100ml (4fl oz) fish stock (see page 219)

100ml (4fl oz) double cream

pinch of cayenne pepper

1 tbsp fresh lemon juice

1 tbsp snipped chives

For the potato purée

1kg (2lb 2oz) floury potatoes, peeled and quartered

75ml (3fl oz) double cream

75ml (3fl oz) milk

50g (2oz) butter

To cook the turbot, place a tiny knob of butter beside each fillet and arrange the tomato vines around the edge. Bake for 10–12 minutes until the topping is crisp, the fish is just cooked through and the tomatoes are beginning to soften.

Meanwhile, finish off the sauce. Pour it into a pan and warm through gently, stirring occasionally, then season with salt and pepper to taste and stir in the lemon juice and chives. Keep warm.

To serve, pipe or spoon the potato purée on to four warmed plates and carefully arrange the crisp turbot fillets on top, then drizzle with the velouté and place a tomato vine to the side of each.

Smoked Salmon Tagliatelle
with Parmesan Cream

Serves 4–6

It's amazing how smoked salmon can make a simple dish so stylish. There is an unwritten rule that says you should never add Parmesan to a fish-based pasta dish, but this recipe is an exception to that rule, as it really works in this cream!

250g (9oz) dried egg tagliatelle

300ml (11fl oz) double cream

6 tbsp freshly grated Parmesan cheese, plus extra to serve

200g (7oz) sliced smoked salmon, thinly sliced into long strips

4 tbsp torn basil, plus extra to garnish

Maldon sea salt and freshly ground black pepper

Cook the tagliatelle in a large saucepan of boiling salted water according to the packet instructions. The bigger the saucepan you use, the less chance there is of the pasta sticking together; it also helps to stir the pasta occasionally.

Pour the cream into a large saucepan, bring to the boil and bubble for 2–3 minutes to allow it to thicken slightly, stirring occasionally. Remove from the heat and stir in the Parmesan cheese (the heat of the cream should melt the cheese), then season with pepper.

Drain the pasta and add to the pan with the Parmesan cream, toss to coat, then fold in the smoked salmon and basil until well combined.

Divide among warmed pasta bowls and garnish with basil leaves. Give each bowl a good grinding of black pepper and serve immediately with the extra grated Parmesan cheese.

Pan-fried Trout
with Crispy Bacon and Garlic

Serves 4

---

8 thin rashers of rindless streaky bacon (dry-cured, if possible)

50g (2oz) seasoned plain flour

8 x 75g (3oz) trout fillets, skinned and boned

100g (4oz) unsalted butter

1 large garlic clove, peeled and crushed

2 tbsp chopped mixed herbs (e.g. flat-leaf parsley, chives and tarragon)

1 lemon

salt and freshly ground black pepper

crushed new potatoes, to serve (see recipe introduction)

This dish is very simple, but when properly executed, it is exquisite. You can use sea trout if available and pancetta (Italian bacon) can be used in place of streaky bacon. Serve with crushed new potatoes – simply steam baby new potatoes until tender, then drain and gently crush each one with a fork. Drizzle with a little olive oil and carefully fold the oil and potatoes together.

Preheat the grill to medium. Arrange the bacon on a grill rack and cook for a minute or so on each side until crisp. Drain the bacon on kitchen paper and allow it to crisp up completely.

Heat a large, heavy-based frying pan over a fairly high heat. Meanwhile, put the seasoned flour on a plate, place each fillet in the flour and coat on both sides, shaking off any surplus. Add 25g (1oz) of the butter to the frying pan and, when it foams, add half the floured trout fillets, presentation-side down. Cook the fillets for 2 minutes until lightly golden, then turn over and cook for another 1–2 minutes depending on the thickness of the fillets. Transfer the cooked fillets to a warmed serving plate, cover loosely with foil and keep warm in an oven on a low heat.

Add another 25g (1oz) of butter to the pan. Cook the rest of the fillets as before, add to the plate with the first batch and keep warm.

Chop or use scissors to snip the cooked bacon rashers. Wipe out the frying pan with some kitchen paper. Add the remaining butter and the garlic to the frying pan and set over a medium heat. When the butter starts to melt and turns to a light brown foam, quickly add the herbs, a good squeeze of lemon juice and salt and pepper to season, swirling the pan to combine.

Arrange two trout fillets on each of four plates and sprinkle the bacon over the fish. Spoon the flavoured butter on top and serve with crushed new potatoes.

Trio of Roast Seafood
with Sun-dried Tomato & Saffron Sauce

This is a delicate, fragrant seafood dish which needs careful and precise cooking. Don't be nervous though, just follow the recipe exactly and the result is well worth it.

To make the sauce, melt the butter in a small saucepan over a medium heat. Add the onion and cook for 2 minutes until soft but not browned, stirring occasionally. Stir in the fish trimmings with the wine, saffron liquid and tomato purée. Simmer on a medium heat for about 5 minutes to reduce by half, then add the sun-dried tomatoes and stock. Bring to the boil and simmer for 10 minutes.

Stir in the cream and simmer for another 10 minutes until reduced by half and thickened. Blitz with a hand-held blender and use the back of a spoon to press the sauce through a fine sieve into a clean pan. Season with salt and pepper to taste, then cover and set aside.

Preheat the oven to 180°C (350°F), gas mark 4 and heat two large frying pans over a medium heat. Season the fish with salt and pepper. Divide the olive oil and most of the butter between the heated pans. When the butter is foaming, add the hake and salmon, skin-side down, to one of the pans. Put the smoked haddock in the second pan, also skin-side down. Gently fry the fish for 2 minutes on each side. Transfer to baking sheets lined with non-stick baking paper and roast in the oven for about 6 minutes until cooked through and tender. Cover loosely with foil and keep warm in a low oven.

Meanwhile, heat a large saucepan over a medium heat. Wash the spinach and shake off any excess water. Add the remaining knob of butter to the pan and then add the spinach, pushing it down to fit in the pan. Stir the spinach until it is wilted and then season with a pinch of salt and the sugar. Drain off any excess water.

To serve, reheat the sauce over a gentle heat and then divide the spinach into small piles on four warmed plates. Drizzle the sauce around the plates and then arrange the fish fillets on the spinach. Garnish each piece of fish with a chervil sprig to serve.

For the seafood

4 x 75g (3oz) hake fillets (about 2.5cm/1in thick), boned but with skin

4 x 75g (3oz) organic salmon fillets (about 2.5cm/1in thick), with skin

4 x 75g (3oz) natural smoked haddock fillets, boned and skinned, about 2.5cm (1in) thick

1 tbsp olive oil

50g (2oz) butter

200g (7oz) spinach, thick stems removed

pinch of caster sugar

Maldon sea salt and freshly ground black pepper

chervil sprigs, to garnish

For the sauce

1 tsp butter, softened

1 small onion, peeled and finely chopped

50g (2oz) fish trimmings

150ml (¼ pint) white wine

large pinch of saffron strands, soaked in 1 tbsp warm water

1 tsp tomato purée

50g (2oz) sun-dried tomatoes, chopped

300ml (11fl oz) vegetable or fish stock (see pages 218–19)

300ml (11fl oz) double cream

Goujons of Lemon Sole
with Chips and Tartare Sauce

Serves 4

Don't just rely on your local takeaway – you can make fish and chips easily at home. Traditionally, they were cooked in pork dripping, which may sound awful, but it really isn't! Fierce battles rage over how to make the perfect batter (as soggy fish is horrid), but my favourite is this Japanese-style tempura batter – light and crisp.

To make the tartare sauce, place the mayonnaise in a bowl and stir in the gherkins, capers, tarragon, parsley, shallot and mustard. Squeeze in enough lemon juice to taste and season generously with salt and pepper. Transfer to a serving bowl, stir to combine, then cover with cling film and chill until ready to serve.

Pour the sunflower oil into a deep-fat fryer or a large deep-sided saucepan, making sure it is only half full, and heat to 170°C (325°F).

Cut the potatoes into chunky chips, about 2cm (¾in) thick, and then place in a bowl of cold water – this helps to remove the starch. Drain and then thoroughly dry them in a clean tea towel. Place the chips in a wire basket (you may need to do this in two batches depending on the size of your basket) and lower them into the hot oil. Cook for 4 minutes until cooked through but not browned. Drain well on kitchen paper and set aside.

Increase the temperature of the sunflower oil to 190°C (375°F) and preheat the oven to 150°C (300°F), gas mark 2.

To make the tempura batter, mix the plain flour and cornflour together in a bowl and then whisk in the iced sparkling water. Season with salt. Do not worry about lumps, as these will improve the texture of the batter, which needs to be used straight away.

Dip the lemon sole strips into the batter and then quickly place in the heated sunflower oil and cook for 4–5 minutes until crisp and golden brown (again, you may have to do this in two batches). Drain on kitchen paper and keep hot in the oven. »

For the tartare sauce

200ml (7fl oz) mayonnaise (see page 209)

2 tbsp baby gherkins (cornichons), finely chopped

1 tbsp capers, rinsed and finely chopped

2 tbsp chopped tarragon

2 tbsp chopped flat-leaf parsley

1 shallot, peeled and finely chopped

1 tsp Dijon mustard

juice of ½ lemon

salt and freshly ground black pepper

For the fish and chips

2 litres (3½ pints) sunflower oil

900g (2lb) floury potatoes (e.g. Désirée or King Edward)

600g (1lb 6oz) lemon sole fillets, skinned and cut into 2.5cm (1in) strips

malt vinegar, to serve

For the tempura batter

50g (2oz) plain flour

50g (2oz) cornflour

175ml (6fl oz) iced sparkling water

Tip the par-cooked chips back into the wire basket and carefully lower into the hot oil. Cook for 1–2 minutes until they are crisp and golden brown. Drain well on kitchen paper and serve immediately with the fish goujons, tartare sauce and vinegar. For an authentic touch, serve the fish and chips on greaseproof paper and wrap in newspaper.

Gratin of Hake, Prawns & Basil
on a bed of Spinach

Serves 4

It might seem like an overload of basil in this dish, but the flavour contrasts beautifully with the fish and the colour looks great. As with most white fish recipes, you can substitute with other round, white fish such as cod or haddock.

Preheat the oven to 180°C (350°F), gas mark 4. Place the hake, skin-side down, on a baking sheet lined with non-stick baking paper and carefully arrange the prawns on top. Sprinkle over the basil and then drizzle the chilli jam or sauce on top. Scatter with mozzarella and season with salt and pepper to taste. Bake for about 15–20 minutes until golden brown.

To sauté the spinach, melt the butter in a medium saucepan over a medium heat. Once it has stopped foaming, quickly sauté the spinach with the sugar until soft and wilted. Season the spinach with salt and pepper to taste and drain well on kitchen paper to remove the excess moisture. Return to the saucepan and keep warm over a very low heat until ready to serve.

Place a pile of the sautéed spinach in the centre of four plates and, using a fish slice, carefully arrange a cooked fillet of hake on top of each. To serve, drizzle 1 tablespoon of pesto around the edge of each plate.

For the hake

4 x 175g (6oz) hake fillets, pin boned and scaled

16 raw Dublin Bay prawns, peeled and veins removed

4 tbsp chopped basil

4 tsp Chilli Jam (see page 215) or sweet chilli sauce

125g (4½oz) grated mozzarella cheese

Maldon sea salt and freshly ground black pepper

4 tbsp Pesto (see page 208)

For the spinach

50g (2oz) butter

225g (8oz) spinach, washed and tough stalks removed

pinch of caster sugar

Thai Seafood Laksa

Serves 4–6

This is a southern Thai dish that I picked up on my travels. The broth has a fragrant, spicy flavour and is great for lunch or as a light dinner. For a variation, you could substitute the seafood with chicken, pork or beef, cut into wafer-thin slices.

Heat a large saucepan over a medium heat. To make the paste, place the chillies in a food processor with the garlic, ginger, ground coriander, fresh coriander and groundnut oil, then blend together to form a coarse paste. Add the paste to the heated pan and stir-fry for 1 minute, then pour in the coconut milk and stock and bring to the boil. Reduce the heat and simmer the sauce for 20 minutes to allow the flavours to combine, stirring occasionally until slightly reduced.

Meanwhile, place the noodles in a large saucepan of boiling salted water and then immediately remove the saucepan from the heat. Set aside for 8–10 minutes (check the packet instructions). Drain and refresh the noodles under cold running water and set them aside.

Blanch the sugar snap peas in a small pan of boiling salted water for 1–2 minutes or until just cooked, then drain and refresh under cold running water. Set aside.

Add the fish sauce to the coconut mixture along with the squid, monkfish and prawns and stir gently for just a few seconds until just cooked through and tender. Add lime juice to taste. Divide the cooked noodles among warmed bowls and scatter the sugar snap peas on top. Ladle over the coconut broth and garnish with the mint and basil leaves, spring onions and chillies to serve.

2 red chillies, halved and deseeded

4 garlic cloves, peeled and roughly chopped

5cm (2in) piece of root ginger, peeled and roughly chopped

1 tsp ground coriander

50g (2oz) bunch of coriander (including stalks)

3 tbsp groundnut oil

2 x 400g tins of coconut milk

900ml (1½ pints) fish, vegetable or chicken stock (see pages 218–19)

225g (8oz) Thai rice noodles

150g (5oz) sugar snap peas

2 tbsp Thai fish sauce (nam pla)

225g (8oz) baby squid, cleaned and washed, cut into rings

225g (8oz) monkfish fillet, skinned and cut into 2.5cm (1in) chunks

12 raw Dublin Bay prawns, peeled and veins removed

juice of 1 lime

salt

handful of shredded mint and basil leaves, thinly sliced spring onions and chopped red chillies, to garnish

Salmon & Spinach En Croute

If you are making these salmon puff pastry parcels more than an hour in advance, dust the bottom layer of pastry with a little semolina or polenta to prevent it going soggy. If using shop-bought pastry, look out for the all-butter variety that is now available in most supermarkets.

Preheat the oven to 200°C (400°F), gas mark 6. Place the butter in a small bowl with the parsley, tarragon, dill, garlic and some salt and cracked black pepper, and stir until well combined. Spoon the butter on to a sheet of cling film or non-stick baking paper and shape into a roll about 2.5cm (1in) thick, wrapping tightly. Chill the butter in the freezer for at least 10 minutes to firm up (or refrigerate for up to 48 hours, if time allows).

Cut the pastry into eight evenly sized sections and roll each out on a lightly floured work surface to a rectangle of 13 x 18cm (5 x 7in), trimming the edges if necessary. Arrange four of the rectangles on baking sheets lined with non-stick baking paper. Place a salmon fillet in the centre of each one.

Unwrap the garlic butter, and cut into 16 equal slices. Arrange four slices on each piece of salmon in an overlapping layer. Cover with the spinach leaves and season with salt and pepper.

Brush the edges of the pastry bases with a little beaten egg and lay a second sheet of pastry on top, pressing down to seal. Crimp all around the edges of each parcel by gently pressing the pastry with the forefinger of one hand and between the first two fingers of the other hand, until completely sealed. Use a sharp knife to make light slashes in the top of each parcel, being careful not to cut right through.

Brush the parcels with the remaining beaten egg and bake for 25–30 minutes until the pastry is cooked through and golden brown. Place on warmed plates with some dressed salad leaves.

Ingredients
100g (4oz) unsalted butter, softened
2 tbsp chopped flat-leaf parsley
1 tbsp chopped tarragon leaves
1 tbsp chopped dill
1 garlic clove, peeled and crushed
500g packet all-butter puff pastry, thawed if frozen
plain flour, for dusting
4 x 175g (6oz) organic salmon fillets (2.5cm/1in thick), skinned and boned
50g (2oz) baby spinach leaves
1 egg, beaten
salt and cracked black pepper
salad leaves lightly dressed with French Vinaigrette (see page 220), to serve

Grilled Plaice and Baby Leeks

with Lemon & Caper Sauce

Serves 4

Homemade stock is best for this lemony sauce, as stock cubes are too salty. Alternatively, use a carton of chilled stock, available from most supermarkets. Heat the sauce gently and don't let it boil, nor let it cool enough for the fat to set – either will result in curdling. To find the best temperature, just stick your finger in – it should feel warm, not hot. For a special occasion, substitute the plaice for Dover sole; otherwise small brill fillets or lemon sole also work well.

300ml (11fl oz) chicken or vegetable stock (see pages 218–19)
4 large plaice fillets, each about 250–275g (9–10oz)
100g (4oz) unsalted butter, diced and chilled
12 baby leeks, trimmed
juice of ½ lemon
1 tbsp snipped chives
2 tbsp capers, rinsed
Maldon sea salt and freshly ground white pepper
boiled baby new potatoes and dressed crisp green salad, to serve

To make the lemon and caper sauce, place the stock in a small saucepan, bring to the boil, then reduce the heat and simmer until it has reduced to about 2 tablespoons.

Preheat the grill to medium. Arrange the plaice fillets on a non-stick baking sheet and dot with a little butter, then season with salt and pepper to taste. Place directly under the grill and cook for 4–5 minutes, without turning, until just through cooked and tender.

Meanwhile, plunge the baby leeks into a large saucepan of boiling salted water and simmer for 2–3 minutes until tender.

When the stock has reduced sufficiently, turn the heat right down to its lowest setting and whisk in the remaining butter (or use a hand-held blender), a few cubes at a time, until it has melted and the texture is light and frothy. Add a squeeze of lemon juice, then stir in the chives and capers. Season with salt and pepper to taste.

Carefully transfer the plaice fillets on to warmed plates using a fish slice. Drain the leeks and arrange alongside. Spoon the sauce on top and serve with boiled baby new potatoes and salad.

Chicken, Lemon & Broccoli Pasta Bake

Serves 6

A pasta bake is always convenient and economical. This one is ideal for using up leftover roast chicken or turkey at Christmas. You can make it with shop-bought cooked chicken as well.

Preheat the oven to 190°C (375°F), gas mark 5. Cook the penne in a large saucepan of boiling salted water according to the packet instructions. Drain well and refresh under cold running water.

Strip the meat off the bones of the chicken and shred or cut into bite-sized pieces – you'll need about 450g (1lb) in total. Place in a bowl and set aside. Blanch the broccoli in a large saucepan of boiling salted water for 2–3 minutes, then drain and refresh under cold running water. Tip on to kitchen paper to drain completely.

Warm the béchamel sauce in a saucepan and whisk in the stock and cream or crème fraîche. Bring to a simmer and then cook for a few minutes, stirring occasionally, until you have achieved a thick pouring sauce – you should have about 500ml (18fl oz) in total. Season with salt and pepper and add enough lemon juice to taste.

Melt the butter in a small saucepan over a medium heat and sauté the onion for 3–4 minutes, then stir in the breadcrumbs, lemon zest and herbs, and season with salt and pepper to taste. Cook for another minute or two until lightly browned. Remove from the heat.

Toss the pasta, cooked chicken pieces and broccoli florets together in a 3.5 litre (6 pint), 5cm (2in) deep, greased ovenproof dish and pour over the sauce to cover completely. Sprinkle the breadcrumb mixture on top and bake for 15–20 minutes or until bubbling and the breadcrumbs are lightly golden. Spoon on to warmed plates and serve at once.

Ingredients
275g (10oz) penne pasta
1 cooked chicken or 450g (1lb) cooked chicken meat
450g (1lb) head of broccoli, cut into bite-sized florets
300ml (11fl oz) Béchamel Sauce (see page 210)
150ml (¼ pint) chicken stock (see page 219)
4 tbsp double cream or crème fraîche
finely grated zest and juice of 1 lemon
25g (1oz) butter, plus extra for greasing
1 small onion, peeled and finely chopped
75g (3oz) fresh white breadcrumbs
2 tbsp chopped flat-leaf parsley
1 tsp chopped sage
salt and freshly ground black pepper

Honey-glazed Peppered Duck Breast
with Sweet Potato Fondant

Serves 4

The sweet potato fondant accompanying this duck is my favourite side dish on the restaurant menu. They're individual little towers, which can be made in advance and reheated on a baking sheet at 180°C (350°F), gas mark 4, for 10 minutes. I normally use a 5cm (2in) cooking ring as a cutter, which creates perfect shapes every time. They are also great served with lamb or beef.

Peel the sweet potatoes and trim down to 10cm (4in) in length. Place the trimmed potatoes on a chopping board and cut each into 2.5cm (1in) slices, then use a straight-sided cutter to stamp out eight 5cm (2in) rounds (keep any scraps to make soup or a purée).

Heat a large frying pan and add the butter and sunflower oil. Add the sweet potato discs and cook for 2–3 minutes on each side until golden. Season with salt and pepper and pour in enough stock to come three-quarters of the way up the potatoes. Add the thyme sprigs. Increase the heat and bring to the boil, then reduce the heat and simmer gently for 15 minutes without moving the potatoes, until the stock mixture has gone and the potatoes are tender when pierced with a sharp knife. Turn the discs over carefully with a spatula. The bottoms will have started to brown and caramelise. Cook for another 3–4 minutes until browned and completely tender.

Meanwhile, preheat the oven to 200°C (400°F), gas mark 6 and the grill to medium. Score the fat on the duck in a criss-cross pattern. Season the duck on both sides with cracked black pepper and salt.

Heat a large, ovenproof frying pan over a medium heat and add the duck breasts, skin-side down (this helps render the duck fat, resulting in a crispy skin) then cook for about 2 minutes until the skin is crisp. Turn the duck breasts over and cook for another minute, then transfer the frying pan to the oven and cook for another 8 minutes for a pink finish or 10 minutes if you prefer them a little more well done. For the last few minutes of the cooking time brush the skin »

For the sweet potato fondants

2 sweet potatoes, each at least 10cm (4in) long and 5cm (2in) across

25g (1oz) butter

1 tsp sunflower oil

300ml (11fl oz) chicken stock (see page 219)

2 sprigs of thyme

Maldon sea salt and freshly ground black pepper

For the duck

4 x 275g (10oz) duck breasts, well trimmed

1 tbsp cracked black pepper

1 tbsp runny honey

chopped coriander, to garnish

100ml (4fl oz) Honey and Clove Sauce or Port and Balsamic Syrup (see pages 212 and 214), to serve

of the duck breasts with the honey, this will give wonderful flavour and caramelise the skin. Once cooked, allow the duck breasts to rest in a warm place for 5 minutes, without covering.

To serve, carve the duck breasts into thin slices, arrange two of the sweet potato fondants on each warmed plate, then drizzle around the Honey and Clove Sauce or Port and Balsamic Syrup, garnish with the coriander and serve immediately.

Pot Roasted Guinea Fowl
with Herby Garlic Butter

Serves 4

Pot roasting is a great way to keep meat succulent and putting it on a bed of vegetables adds loads of flavour. Serve with a dollop of creamy mash. This recipe also works very well with chicken breasts.

Preheat the oven to 170°C (325°F), gas mark 3. To make the garlic butter, place the butter in a mini blender with the garlic, herbs and salt and pepper. Blend briefly and transfer to a small bowl with a spatula. Chill until needed.

Heat a flameproof casserole dish with a lid over a medium heat. Add the olive oil to the dish and then add the guinea fowl breasts, skin-side down. Cook for a few minutes on each side until golden brown. Transfer to a plate.

Add the leek, carrots, celery and thyme to the casserole dish and sauté for about 5 minutes, over a medium heat, until just starting to soften but not to brown. Add the wine and stock and allow to bubble a little, then arrange the browned guinea fowl on top with any juices from the plate. Cover the casserole dish with the lid and bake in the oven for 15–20 minutes or until the guinea fowl is tender.

Transfer the guinea fowl to a warmed plate. Whisk two-thirds of the garlic butter into the vegetable mixture left in the casserole dish and divide among warmed plates. Arrange the guinea fowl over the vegetables and top each with a quarter of the remaining garlic butter. Serve with a warmed bowl of creamy mashed potatoes.

75g (3oz) unsalted butter, at room temperature

2 garlic cloves, peeled and crushed

2 tbsp chopped mixed herbs (e.g. flat-leaf parsley, tarragon and basil)

1 tbsp olive oil

4 corn-fed guinea fowl breast fillets, skin on

1 large leek, trimmed and finely chopped

2 carrots, peeled and diced

3 celery sticks, diced

1 tsp chopped thyme

6 tbsp dry white wine

3 tbsp chicken stock (see page 219)

salt and freshly ground black pepper

Creamy Mashed Potatoes, to serve (see page 217)

Duck Confit

with Savoy Cabbage & Red Onion Sauté

Serves 6

Confit is a traditional French way of cooking duck. The method is centuries-old – first the meat is cured in salt, then poached in its own fat. Be prepared that this special recipe does take a while, but it's definitely worth it. You'll need about 1 litre (1¾ pints) of duck fat, available from your butcher or larger supermarkets. If you don't have enough, combine with peanut oil or chicken fat, or just use either of those instead. In the restaurant we keep the fat from any duck carcasses and freeze it in plastic bags. Then I take it out as needed, simmer in water to render it, and strain through a seive before using.

For the duck

6 duck legs

1 garlic clove, peeled and sliced

6 whole star anise

4 tbsp coarse sea salt

6–7 sprigs of thyme

1 orange, sliced and pips removed

1 litre (1¾ pints) duck fat, peanut oil or chicken fat (see recipe introduction)

Honey and Clove Sauce, to serve (optional, see page 212)

For the cabbage and onion

75g (3oz) unsalted butter

1 tbsp olive oil

1 red onion, peeled and thinly sliced

1 garlic clove, peeled and thinly chopped

175g (6oz) Savoy cabbage, core removed and thinly sliced

salt and freshly ground black pepper

To marinate the duck legs, place in a single layer in a shallow non-metallic dish and scatter over the garlic, star anise, sea salt and thyme sprigs. Cover the dish with cling film. Place in the fridge overnight to allow the flavours to penetrate the duck.

Preheat the oven to 100°C (225°F), gas mark ¼. Rinse the marinade off the duck legs and pat them dry with kitchen paper. Return the duck legs to the dish and scatter the orange slices on top.

Heat the duck fat gently in a saucepan, then pour it over the duck legs (if the fat does not completely cover the legs, top it up with the peanut oil or chicken fat). Place in the oven and cook the duck for about 4 hours until it is tender and the meat is almost falling from the bone. Remove from the heat and allow to cool in the fat. This can be made up to 3 days in advance and stored in the fridge.

When ready to serve, preheat the grill to low. Remove the duck and orange slices from the fat and brush off any excess. Arrange the legs on a grill rack, skin-side up and nestle six orange slices around them. Don't put the rack too close to the grill or the skin will burn. Cook for 10–15 minutes until the duck skin is crisp and golden. Turn the orange slices halfway through; they should be just catching colour. »

Meanwhile, cook the cabbage. Place the butter and olive oil in a large saucepan and once the butter is foaming, add the onion and garlic. Sauté over a fairly high heat for 2–3 minutes until it is lightly browned, tossing occasionally. Add the cabbage and cook for a further 3–4 minutes, adding 2–3 tablespoons of water if necessary, until just tender but still crunchy. Season the cabbage with salt and pepper to taste and keep warm.

To serve, divide the Savoy cabbage and red onion mixture among warmed plates and arrange the crispy duck confit on top, place the caramelised orange slices to the side and drizzle the Honey and Clove Sauce around, if using.

Coq au Vin

Serves 6

A classic French Coq au Vin is made with a cock bird, but I make a less authentic version from chicken legs, delicious nonetheless. If you want to go all-out on the presentation, garnish the finished dish with heart-shaped croûtons. Simply stamp or cut out heart shapes from sliced white bread and fry in a little oil until golden brown. Remove from the pan with tongs and immediately dip the pointed ends into chopped parsley.

Season the chicken all over with salt and pepper. Heat 1 tablespoon of the sunflower oil, in a flameproof casserole dish with a lid, over a medium heat. Add the bacon and sauté for 3–4 minutes until lightly browned, stirring occasionally. Remove the bacon using a slotted spoon and place in a bowl. Set aside.

Add half the seasoned chicken legs to the casserole dish, presentation-side down and cook for 3–4 minutes over a medium heat until they are golden brown, turning occasionally. Transfer to a plate and repeat with the remaining chicken legs.

Increase the heat a little and add another tablespoon of oil if necessary. Add the onion to the casserole dish with the carrots, »

6 chicken legs
1–2 tbsp sunflower oil
175g (6oz) piece of smoked bacon, rind removed and meat cut into strips
1 onion, peeled and sliced
2 carrots, peeled and sliced
2 celery sticks, sliced
2 garlic cloves, peeled and finely chopped
1 bottle of red wine
2 tsp chopped thyme leaves
500ml (18fl oz) chicken stock (see page 219)
25g (1oz) butter
18 baby onions or small shallots
250g (9oz) button mushrooms, quartered
2 tsp cornflour
salt and freshly ground black pepper
chopped flat-leaf parsley and heart shaped croûtons, to garnish (optional, see recipe introduction)
Roasted Root Vegetables, to serve (see page 217)

celery and garlic and sauté for about 5 minutes until they are golden brown, stirring occasionally. Pour in the red wine, add the thyme and bring to a simmer, then cook for 5 minutes, scraping the bottom of the pan with a wooden spoon to remove any sediment. Pour in the stock and return the chicken legs to the pan. Bring to a simmer, then cover and simmer gently for about 45 minutes or until the chicken is cooked through and completely tender.

Meanwhile, melt the butter in a frying pan over a medium heat. Add the baby onions or shallots and sauté for 5 minutes, shaking the pan occasionally. Scoop the onions out with a slotted spoon and add to the bowl with the reserved bacon. Tip the mushrooms into the pan and sauté for about 5 minutes until tender. Add the mushrooms to the bacon and onion mixture and set aside.

When the chicken legs are cooked, use a slotted spoon to carefully transfer them to a large plate, then set aside. Strain the sauce into a large clean saucepan, discarding the vegetables. Mix the cornflour with a little water, then whisk it into the sauce. Bring the sauce to the boil and then reduce the heat to a simmer and cook for a few minutes until thickened, whisking occasionally. Stir in the bacon, onion and mushroom mixture and simmer for 6–8 minutes until heated through, so that the flavours have had a chance to combine. Return the chicken to the casserole, nestling it into the sauce and simmer for another 5 minutes until heated through. Season with salt and pepper to taste.

To serve, transfer the Coq au Vin to a warmed serving dish and sprinkle over the parsley. Garnish with the heart-shaped croûtons, if you wish, and serve straight from the table on to warmed plates. Serve the roasted root vegetables in a separate warmed dish as an accompaniment.

Roast Chicken
with Lemon, Garlic and Thyme

There is something very momentous about a whole roast chicken being brought to the table – it always reminds me of family Sunday lunches. The flavours in this dish are fantastic and really penetrate the flesh of the chicken.

1.5kg (3lb 4oz) chicken (preferably free-range or organic)
I lemon
I sprig of thyme
75g (3oz) butter, softened
2 garlic cloves, peeled and crushed
2 red onions, peeled and halved
4 small carrots, peeled
I leek, chopped in half
2 celery sticks, chopped in half
I garlic bulb, broken into cloves (but not peeled)
3 tbsp olive oil
I tbsp plain flour
100ml (4fl oz) white wine
600ml (1 pint) chicken or vegetable stock (see pages 218–19)
salt and freshly ground black pepper
roast potatoes and buttered peas, to serve

Take the chicken out of the fridge 30 minutes in advance. Preheat the oven to 230°C (450°F), gas mark 8. Finely grate the zest from the lemon and place it in a bowl, reserving the rest of the lemon. Strip the thyme leaves from the stalks (reserve the stalks) and add to the lemon zest. Mix in the butter and the garlic and then season with salt and pepper.

Loosen the skin from the chicken breasts, starting at the cavity end and working your hand underneath to release it. Spread the garlic butter evenly under the skin and lay the skin back down on top. Slash the chicken legs several times with a sharp knife (this is to help ensure that the skin crisps up while the chicken cooks).

Place the onions in a roasting tin with the carrots, leek, celery and garlic cloves, tossing to coat in 1 tablespoon of olive oil. Sit the chicken on top of the pile of vegetables and drizzle all over with the remaining olive oil, then season well, rubbing it all over and right into the slashes.

Cut the reserved lemon in half and put both halves inside the chicken's cavity with the reserved thyme stalks. Place the chicken in the oven and immediately reduce the heat to 200°C (400°F), gas mark 6. Roast the chicken for 1 hour 20 minutes, basting it halfway through cooking.

When the chicken is cooked, remove from the oven and transfer to a board. Put the carrots and red onions on a warmed plate. Cover the chicken and the vegetables with foil and set aside for 15 minutes while you make the gravy. »

Using a large spoon, carefully remove most of the fat from the tin and then place the tin directly on the heat. Stir in the flour and, holding the tin steady, mash the remaining vegetables as much as possible with a potato masher to release their juices. Pour the wine into the tin and allow it to bubble, stirring continuously to blend in the flour. Pour in the stock and bring to the boil, then reduce the heat and simmer for about 10 minutes, stirring occasionally, until slightly reduced and thickened. Take a large jug and set a sieve above it, then pour in the gravy mixture and push some of the vegetable fibres through with the back of the spoon. Stir in the juices from the resting chicken and season with salt and pepper to taste. Transfer to a warmed gravy boat.

Carve the chicken into slices and arrange on warmed plates with the reserved carrots and red onion halves, the roast potatoes and buttered peas. Serve with the gravy.

Masala Chicken Meatballs

These delicious balls make good use of versatile chicken mince and are bursting with ginger, cumin and coriander. You can also make them using turkey mince with equally successful results.

Place the chicken mince in a bowl with the ginger, cumin seeds, onion, coriander, a teaspoon of salt and a good grinding of pepper. Mix until combined, then, with dampened hands, divide into 20 evenly sized balls. Place on a plate, cover with cling film and refrigerate until needed.

To make the sauce, heat the sunflower oil in a large saucepan, wide enough to fit the meatballs in a single layer. Add the cumin seeds, cloves and bay leaf. When the mixture starts sizzling, add the onions and garlic, stirring to combine. Cover and cook on a very low heat for 10 minutes, stirring occasionally.

Stir the sauce well, increase the heat and fry for another 8–10 minutes until dried out and just beginning to brown, stirring occasionally. Reduce the heat and stir in the passata, chillies, ginger, garam masala and turmeric, then cook for another 4–5 minutes. Add 350ml (12fl oz) of boiling water, stir well and season with salt and pepper. Use a hand-held blender to whiz the sauce until as smooth as possible, tilting the pan slightly and being careful of splattering. Return to a simmer, add the meatballs, cover and simmer on a low heat for 30 minutes. Gently shake the pan occasionally to ensure the meatballs are not sticking to the base of the pan, but do not stir.

Turn the meatballs over, then sprinkle with the tandoori masala powder and sugar. Shake the pan gently and continue to cook with no lid for 5 minutes until the sauce has thickened slightly.

Divide the meatballs and sauce among warmed bowls, add a dollop of soured cream, and garnish with chopped coriander. Serve at once with your choice of rice, chapattis or naan bread.

For the meatballs

450g (1lb) chicken mince

2 tsp freshly grated root ginger

1 tsp cumin seeds

1 small onion, peeled, grated and squeezed dry

2 tbsp chopped coriander, plus extra to garnish

salt and freshly ground black pepper

soured cream, basmati rice and warm chapattis or naan bread, to serve

For the sauce

4 tbsp sunflower oil

1 tsp cumin seeds

2 whole cloves

1 bay leaf

2 onions, peeled and roughly chopped

4 garlic cloves, peeled and roughly chopped

150ml (¼ pint) passata (sieved tomatoes)

3 green chillies, deseeded and finely chopped

2 tsp freshly grated root ginger

1 tsp garam masala

2 tsp turmeric

½ tsp tandoori masala powder

pinch of caster sugar

Chicken Pad Thai Noodles

Serves 4

The best Pad Thai I ever ate was while sitting in a rickety chair on a Bangkok pavement. The aroma of all the wonderful ingredients was sensational and the flavour just blew me away! Here's my version.

Place the shrimps in a small bowl, cover with boiling water and allow to soak for 10 minutes. Blend the roasted peanuts in a mini food processor or roughly grind using a pestle and mortar.

Cook the noodles in a saucepan of boiling water according to the packet instructions and then drain well. Mix the lime juice, sugar, rice vinegar, soy sauce, Thai fish sauce and chillies together in a small bowl, stirring to dissolve the sugar and set aside.

Heat 2 tablespoons of oil in a wok until very hot, then stir-fry the chicken for 6–8 minutes until cooked through and just turning golden. Remove from the pan and cover loosely with foil to keep warm. Pour in the beaten eggs and quickly swirl the wok so that the egg sticks to the sides in a thin layer. Leave for about 30 seconds until the egg is just set, then break into small pieces with a wooden spoon. Remove and set aside with the chicken.

Wipe the wok with kitchen paper and return it to a medium heat, adding the remaining tablespoon of oil. Stir-fry the shallots and garlic for 2–3 minutes until softened and just beginning to brown. Drain the dried shrimps and add them to the wok, stir-frying for 30 seconds. Pour the lime juice mixture into the wok and simmer for 1–2 minutes until it has reduced and thickened slightly.

Add the noodles, beansprouts, spring onions and coriander to the wok, toss for 1 minute to wilt the beansprouts, then return the cooked chicken and egg to the pan, and toss everything to combine.

Serve the Pad Thai noodles in warmed bowls, garnish with sprigs of coriander, and place the lime wedges and a little pile of the ground peanuts to one side.

Ingredients
1 tbsp dried shrimps
100g (4oz) roasted peanuts
175g (6oz) flat rice noodles
juice of 2 limes
1 tbsp palm sugar or light muscovado sugar
2 tsp rice vinegar
2 tsp dark soy sauce
3 tbsp Thai fish sauce (nam pla)
1–2 red bird's eye chillies, finely sliced
3 tbsp peanut oil
2 skinless chicken breast fillets, thinly sliced
2 eggs, beaten
2 shallots, peeled and finely sliced
2 garlic cloves, peeled and finely chopped
200g (7oz) beansprouts
4 spring onions, trimmed and thinly sliced
2 tbsp roughly chopped coriander, plus sprigs of coriander, to garnish
lime wedges, to serve

Stuffed Roast Goose

with Braised Red Cabbage and Smoked Bacon

Serves 8

This is what we always eat for our family Christmas dinner, served with all the trimmings. Free-range geese are now in plentiful supply during the festive period, so if you've not tried goose before, give it a go – you can't beat it! Make sure you save the drained-off fat and use it to make crispy roast potatoes. I normally make my red cabbage the day before, and it also freezes well.

To make the stuffing, heat the olive oil in a large frying pan over a medium heat. Add the apple slices and sauté for 3–4 minutes until soft and golden. Transfer to a bowl and allow to cool. Once cool, add the thyme, sausage meat, breadcrumbs, cranberries and walnuts, stirring gently to evenly mix. Season with salt and pepper to taste.

Preheat the oven to 200°C (400°F), gas mark 6. Place the goose on a rack set over a roasting tin (so that any fat drains off during cooking). Pour a kettleful of boiling water over the goose (this helps loosen the fat from the skin), then drain off the water from the tin. To stuff the goose, start at the neck end where you'll find a flap of loose skin – gently ease this up and away from the breast to open a triangular pocket. Pack two-thirds of the stuffing in as deep as possible and pat into a neat round shape on the outside, then fold the neck flap back down over the stuffing, tuck it under the goose and secure with a small skewer. Rub the goose all over with salt.

Press the remaining stuffing into a 225g (8oz) loaf tin and set aside. Weigh the goose and calculate the cooking time, allowing 15 minutes per 450g (1lb), plus 15 minutes – this goose should take about 3½ hours. Place the goose (on the rack over the tin) in the oven to roast, draining off the excess fat every 30 minutes. After an hour, reduce the oven temperature to 180°C (350°F), gas mark 4. Continue to cook, still draining the fat off every 30 minutes. »

For the goose

6kg (13lb) oven-ready goose, at room temperature

2 tbsp redcurrant jelly

1 tbsp balsamic vinegar

1 tbsp ruby red port or red wine

finely grated zest of 1 orange

salt and freshly ground black pepper

sprigs of thyme, to garnish

Madeira Sauce or Red Wine Sauce (see page 211 or 210), to serve

For the stuffing

2 tbsp olive oil

2 eating apples, peeled, cored and cut into thin slices

1 tbsp chopped thyme

350g (12oz) quality sausage meat

75g (3oz) fresh white breadcrumbs

100g (4oz) dried cranberries

100g (4oz) walnut halves, chopped

For the red cabbage

1 tbsp sunflower oil

50g (2oz) rindless smoked bacon, diced

1 medium red cabbage, core removed and finely sliced

2 tbsp balsamic vinegar

4 tbsp light muscovado sugar

300ml (11fl oz) red wine

300ml (11fl oz) apple juice

2 cooking apples, peeled, cored and chopped

1 tsp each of ground cinnamon, ground cloves and mixed spice

Meanwhile, prepare the red cabbage. Heat the sunflower oil in a heavy-based saucepan over a high heat. Add the bacon and sauté for 30 seconds, then add the cabbage, stirring to combine.

Reduce the heat and cook for 15 minutes until the cabbage is well cooked down, adding a tablespoon or two of water if the cabbage starts to catch on the bottom. Add the balsamic vinegar, sugar, red wine and apple juice. Give everything a good stir, then cover with a lid and simmer for 1 hour over a low heat, stirring occasionally. Stir in the apples and spices and cook gently for another 30 minutes, again stirring occasionally. Season with salt and pepper to taste and keep warm over a low heat.

Remove the goose from the oven 30 minutes before the end of the cooking time. Warm the redcurrant jelly, balsamic vinegar, port or wine and orange zest in a small saucepan. Bring to a simmer, stirring until the jelly dissolves, and then cook for 4–5 minutes until syrupy. Brush all over the goose. Return the goose to the oven, along with the reserved tin of extra stuffing, and cook for the final 30 minutes until the goose is completely tender. Transfer the goose to a serving platter and cover with foil, then allow to rest for 20 minutes. Remove the stuffing from the goose, using a spoon, and transfer to a warmed bowl. Turn out the tin of extra stuffing into the same bowl.

To serve, garnish the roast goose with the thyme and bring to the table. Carve the goose into slices and arrange on warmed plates, discarding any excess fat. Add some of the stuffing to each plate, and some of the braised red cabbage. Serve the Madeira Sauce or Red Wine Sauce in a jug to accompany the goose.

Venison Bourguignon

Serves 4–6

Another French classic, this dish is cooked in the Burgundy style – with red wine. I learned to make it at college and it has been part of my repertoire ever since. The easiest way to peel shallots is to place them in a heatproof bowl and pour over enough boiling water to cover. Set aside until cool enough to handle, then drain, and the skin will come right off.

Preheat the oven to 180°C (350°F), gas mark 4. Heat 1 tablespoon of olive oil and half the butter in a flameproof casserole dish with a lid. Season the flour with salt and pepper and place it in a shallow bowl with the paprika, mixing to combine. Lightly dust the venison in the flour, shaking off any excess. Add the floured venison to the casserole, in small batches, and cook over a high heat for 2–3 minutes until lightly browned. Transfer the meat to a plate and repeat until all the meat has been sealed. Set the meat aside.

Add the remaining olive oil and butter to the casserole dish, stir in the shallots and smoked bacon and cook for 2–3 minutes over a medium heat, stirring, until the shallots are lightly browned and the bacon is golden, adding the garlic in the last 30 seconds. Pour in the wine and allow to bubble for 1–2 minutes, scraping the sediment from the bottom, then stir in the beef stock and tomato purée. Return the meat and juices to the casserole and bring to the boil, then add the thyme and bay leaf. Season with salt and pepper, cover with the lid and transfer to the oven for 2 hours until the venison is almost tender and cooked through.

Remove the casserole from the oven. Stir in the carrots and mushrooms and return to the oven to cook for another 30 minutes or until the venison and vegetables are completely tender. Season with salt and pepper to taste.

Place some mashed potato in the centre of warmed wide-rimmed bowls and spoon the venison bourguignon over the top. Garnish with parsley, if you wish, and serve at once.

Ingredients
2 tbsp olive oil
25g (1oz) butter
25g (1oz) plain flour
2 tsp paprika
1kg (2lb 2oz) venison haunch or shoulder, trimmed and cut into 1cm (½in) cubes
225g (8oz) baby shallots, peeled and halved (keep the roots intact)
100g (4oz) rindless smoked bacon, finely chopped
1 garlic clove, peeled and crushed
300ml (11fl oz) red wine
900ml (1½ pints) beef stock (see page 218)
1 tbsp tomato purée
1 tbsp chopped thyme leaves
1 bay leaf
100g (4oz) carrots, peeled and diced
75g (3oz) button mushrooms, wiped clean
salt and freshly ground black pepper
chopped flat-leaf parsley, to garnish (optional)
Creamy Mashed Potato, to serve (see page 217)

Braised Beef Cheek

with Smoked Bacon, Baby Mushrooms and Celeriac Mash

Beef cheeks are the most tender cut of meat you'll ever taste! They are a favourite of mine and very popular with my regular customers. Ask your local butcher for them, as they're not widely available. The butcher can trim the meat for you, or to do it yourself, remove the top flap of meat and the silver skin from the bottom. The celeriac mash can be made a day ahead and reheated gently with a knob of butter.

Preheat the oven to 170°C (325°F), gas mark 3. Heat 1 tablespoon of oil in a large, flameproof casserole (with a lid) over a medium heat. Add the pieces of beef and brown all over for 4–5 minutes, turning regularly with tongs. Transfer to a plate. Add another tablespoon of oil to the casserole, reduce the heat a little and add the carrots, onion and garlic. Cook for a further 5 minutes, stirring, until golden brown.

Return the beef and any juices to the casserole dish and pour over the red wine and beef stock. Add the herbs and season with salt and pepper to taste, then bring to the boil. Cover the dish tightly with foil and a lid. Cook in the oven for 3 hours until the beef is really tender and melting.

Carefully remove the beef cheeks from the braising juices, allow to rest on a warmed plate and cover loosely with foil. Strain the cooking juices into a medium saucepan and allow them to simmer rapidly for 40–45 minutes until reduced by a quarter.

Meanwhile, make the celeriac mash. Cut the top and bottom off the celeriac, cut it into quarters and, using a small, sharp knife or vegetable peeler, peel away the thick, knobbly skin. Cut it into 1cm (½in) chunks and place in a large saucepan with the potatoes. Pour over the milk, bring to the boil, then reduce the heat and simmer for 15–20 minutes or until the vegetables are completely tender.

Drain the cooked vegetables in a colander set over a bowl to catch the cooking liquid. Tip the cooked vegetables into a food processor »

For the beef cheeks

4 tbsp olive oil

4 x 250g (9oz) pieces beef cheek, well trimmed

2 carrots, peeled and cut into chunks

1 onion, peeled and roughly chopped

2 garlic cloves, peeled and crushed

600ml (1 pint) red wine

1.2 litres (2 pints) beef stock (see page 218)

2 thyme sprigs

2 rosemary sprigs

150g (5oz) piece of smoked bacon, rind removed and diced

150g (5oz) button mushrooms, wiped clean

Maldon sea salt and freshly ground white pepper

chopped flat-leaf parsley, to garnish

For the celeriac mash

½ celeriac (about 500g/1lb 2oz)

275g (10oz) floury potatoes, cut into 1cm (½in) chunks

600ml (1 pint) milk

25g (1oz) butter

along with the butter, and whiz for a few minutes until you have achieved a smooth purée, adding some of the reserved cooking liquid if necessary to give a soft dropping consistency. Season with salt and pepper to taste. Keep warm over a very low heat.

Meanwhile, heat a large, non-stick frying pan over a medium heat. Add the remaining oil and sauté the bacon and mushrooms for 4–5 minutes until golden brown. Drain off any excess oil and stir into the reduced braising juices. Season with salt and pepper to taste.

Divide the celeriac mash among wide-rimmed bowls and carefully arrange the cooked beef cheeks on top. Ladle over the braising juice with the bacon and mushrooms. Garnish with parsley to serve.

Venison Steaks
with Stewed Plums and Roasted Garlic Mash

Serves 4

I love venison and think it's vastly underrated. I have used fillet steaks in this recipe, which, unlike fillet beef steaks, are actually cut from the sirloin that runs the length of the deer. They are far superior to any other cut. Rump or topside can be substituted, but need a little more cooking time as they aren't as tender and so are usually roasted or used in casseroles. For hundreds of years, venison was stored by burying it underground, but thankfully these days it is stored or hung in much the same way as beef!

8 garlic cloves, unpeeled
4 tbsp olive oil
900g (2lb) floury potatoes, cut into 2.5cm (1in) cubes
75ml (3fl oz) ruby red port or red wine
1 tbsp balsamic vinegar
2 tbsp light muscovado sugar
1 tsp chopped thyme leaves, plus sprigs to garnish
4 large plums, halved, stoned and quartered
4 x 150g (5oz) venison fillet steaks
50g (2oz) unsalted butter
about 2 tbsp milk
salt and freshly ground black pepper

Place the garlic and 2 tablespoons of the olive oil in a small frying pan and cook over a very low heat for 8–10 minutes until the garlic cloves are completely tender and lightly golden, tossing occasionally. Remove from the heat, scoop out the garlic with a slotted spoon and place on a plate, then set aside to cool.

Place the potatoes in a large saucepan of boiling salted water, cover and simmer for 10–12 minutes or until completely tender.

Meanwhile, pour the port or red wine into a medium saucepan with the balsamic vinegar, sugar and thyme. »

Heat gently for a couple of minutes until the sugar has dissolved, stirring occasionally. Tip in the plums, bring to a simmer and cook for 5–8 minutes or until the plums are softened but still holding their shape – the time will depend on their ripeness.

Heat a large, heavy-based frying pan until very hot. Rub the remaining 2 tablespoons of olive oil all over the venison steaks and season with salt and pepper. Add the steaks to the heated pan and cook for 2 minutes, then turn over and cook for another 3 minutes for rare venison. If you prefer your steak cooked medium, increase the cooking time by 1 minute on each side; or for well-done, increase the cooking time by 2 minutes on each side. Remove the steaks from the heat, cover and set aside in a warm place to rest for about 5 minutes.

Drain the potatoes and mash them until they are smooth, then beat in the butter and add enough milk to make a smooth purée. Squeeze the pulp from the cooled garlic cloves into a small bowl and mash it with a fork until smooth and creamy. Stir the mashed garlic into the mashed potatoes. Beat the mash well until the potatoes and garlic are well combined. Season with salt and pepper to taste.

Carve the venison steaks into slices and arrange on four warmed serving plates with a pile of the roasted garlic mash. Spoon the stewed plums over the venison, garnish with the thyme sprigs and serve immediately.

Toulouse Sausages

with Creamy Apple & Potato Mash and Red Onion Gravy

Serves 4

This is an extra-special version of sausage and mash, made with Toulouse sausages – a mildly spiced French speciality. I have an excellent local supplier who gets me the most wonderful ones. However, any good-quality sausage works well instead.

To make the gravy, melt the butter in a large frying pan, add the onions and sugar, and cook over a medium heat for 20–30 minutes until caramelised, stirring occasionally. Pour in the wine and allow it to bubble down and then simmer for about 4–5 minutes until it has almost disappeared. Stir in the flour and cook for 1 minute, stirring. Gradually stir in the stock, then season with salt and pepper to taste and simmer gently for 4–5 minutes until you have a thick, rich gravy. Keep warm over a low heat.

Meanwhile, make the mash. Place the potatoes in a large saucepan of boiling salted water and simmer for 15–20 minutes until tender. After the potatoes have been cooking for 10 minutes, heat the sunflower oil in a frying pan and cook the sausages for about 10 minutes or until they are golden brown and cooked through, turning regularly.

Place 25g (1oz) of the butter in a small saucepan with the diced apple and cook gently for 4–5 minutes until the apple is completely soft, stirring occasionally and then mash it down with a fork.

Drain the potatoes and mash them until they are smooth. Heat the milk and the remaining butter in a small saucepan. Beat the hot milk mixture and the apple mixture into the mashed potatoes. Season with salt and pepper to taste.

Divide the apple-flavoured mash among warmed plates and arrange the sausages alongside. Spoon the onion gravy over the sausages. Garnish with parsley and add a good dollop of Dijon mustard to each plate to serve.

For the sausages and mash

900g (2lb) floury potatoes, peeled and cut into chunks

1 tbsp sunflower oil

8 large Toulouse pork sausages

75g (3oz) butter

1 crisp eating apple, peeled, cored and diced

100ml (3½fl oz) milk

Maldon sea salt and freshly ground black pepper

chopped flat-leaf parsley, to garnish

Dijon mustard, to serve

For the red onion gravy

25g (1oz) butter

450g (1lb) red onions, peeled, halved and thinly sliced

½ tsp light muscovado sugar

150ml (¼ pint) red wine

1 tbsp plain flour

300ml (11fl oz) beef stock (see page 218)

Wild Boar Sausage Cassoulet

Serves 4

Wild boar sausages are available to buy from butchers and larger supermarkets, but if you can't find them, you can use any type of good-quality sausages for this recipe. An authentic cassoulet is a rich, slow-cooked bean stew or casserole originating from the south of France. It contains meat (normally sausages, pork, goose, duck or sometimes mutton), pork skin and white haricot beans. If you can't find haricot beans, cannellini beans are the best alternative. The dish is actually named after the 'cassole', the deep, round, earthenware pot with slanting sides in which it is traditionally cooked. This, however, is a much simpler version – the end result tastes nearly as good but with much less effort! I hope you enjoy it.

4 tbsp olive oil

8 large wild boar sausages

1 large onion, peeled and finely chopped

2 celery sticks, finely chopped

2 garlic cloves, peeled and finely chopped

1 red chilli, deseeded and finely chopped

1 tbsp chopped sage

2 x 400g tins of chopped tomatoes

400g tin of haricot beans, drained and rinsed

1 tsp smoked paprika

Maldon sea salt and freshly ground black pepper

chopped flat-leaf parsley, to garnish

crusty bread and Creamy Mashed Potatoes (see page 217), to serve

Preheat the oven to 180°C (350°F), gas mark 4. Heat 1 tablespoon of the olive oil in a large, heavy-based frying pan. Add the sausages and cook gently for 1–2 minutes or until they are just sealed and lightly browned on all sides. Transfer the sausages to a plate and set aside until needed.

Wipe out the frying pan and then add the remaining 3 tablespoons of olive oil. Add the onion, celery, garlic, chilli and sage and then sauté very gently for about 10 minutes until the onion is completely softened but not browned, stirring occasionally. Add the tomatoes and bring to a simmer, then cook for about 10 minutes, stirring occasionally, until the sauce is slightly reduced and thickened. Season with salt and pepper to taste.

Transfer the tomato mixture to a small roasting tin or casserole dish – the mixture needs to fit quite snugly. Then stir in the haricot beans and smoked paprika and arrange the sausages on top, burying them down into the mixture. Roast for 20–25 minutes until the cassoulet is bubbling and the sausages are cooked through and tender. Scatter the parsley over and serve straight away with mashed potatoes and a basket of crusty bread.

Rib-Eye Steaks

with Wild Mushroom Butter and Potato Gratin

Serves 4

This recipe uses my favourite cut of beef, the rib-eye, which is nice and tender but with enough fat and texture to give a great result. When cooking steak, it's best to bring the meat to room temperature first, so I remove the steaks from the fridge 30 minutes before cooking. To make the wild mushroom butter extra special I like to add a teaspoon of white truffle oil.

A day ahead, trim the rib-eye steaks of any excess fat, place in a non-metallic dish and add the olive oil, garlic and thyme, tossing to coat. Cover with cling film and leave in the fridge overnight to marinate if time allows.

To make the mushroom-flavoured butter, heat the olive oil in a small saucepan over a low heat and add the garlic, shallot and mushrooms. Cook gently for 5 minutes until cooked through and tender but not browned. Stir in the Maderia, cream and herbs and cook for a further 3 minutes until the liquid has completely reduced and evaporated. Season with salt and pepper to taste and allow to cool completely.

Place the diced butter and cooked wild mushroom mixture in a food processor and purée until smooth. Using a spatula, scrape out on to a square of non-stick baking paper and roll into a cylinder that is about 2.5cm (1in) thick, twisting the ends to secure. Chill in the fridge for at least 2 hours until solid, or for up to 48 hours. It can also be frozen for up to 1 month.

On the day of your meal, make the potato gratin. Slice the potatoes into wafer thin slices and preheat the oven to 160°C (325°F), gas mark 3. Pour the milk and cream into a small saucepan and add the garlic and nutmeg. Season with salt and pepper to taste and just heat through but do not allow the mixture to boil, then quickly remove from the heat. »

For the steaks

4 x 225g (8oz) dry aged rib-eye steaks (for more info see page 30)

100ml (3½fl oz) olive oil

2 garlic cloves, peeled and crushed

1 tsp chopped thyme leaves

salt and freshly ground black pepper

mixed green salad, dressed with French Vinaigrette (see page 220), to serve

For the mushroom butter

1 tbsp olive oil

1 garlic clove, peeled and crushed

1 shallot, peeled and finely diced

50g (2oz) mixed wild mushrooms (e.g. cep, chanterelle, shiitake and oyster), roughly chopped if large

1 tbsp Maderia

1 tbsp double cream

½ tsp chopped thyme leaves

1 tsp chopped flat-leaf parsley

100g (4oz) butter, diced, at room temperature

For the potato gratin

900g (2lb) potatoes

400ml (14fl oz) milk

300ml (11fl oz) double cream

4 garlic cloves, peeled and crushed

good pinch of freshly grated nutmeg

8 rashers of rindless smoked streaky bacon

butter, for greasing

50g (2oz) Cheddar cheese, grated

Meanwhile, preheat the grill to medium. Arrange the bacon rashers on a grill rack and cook for about 5 minutes until crisp and lightly golden, turning once. Drain on kitchen paper and, when cool enough to handle, snip into pieces with scissors.

Grease a 23 x 18cm (9 x 7in) ovenproof dish, of 5cm (2in) in depth, with the butter and arrange a third of the potato slices in the base of the dish. Season with salt and pepper to taste and scatter over half of the bacon, then add another third of the potatoes in an even layer, season again and scatter over the remaining bacon. Arrange the rest of the potatoes on top in an attractive, overlapping layer and carefully pour over the milk mixture.

Cover the potato gratin with foil and place the dish on a baking sheet. Bake for 1¼ hours or until cooked through and lightly golden, then remove the foil. Sprinkle over the grated Cheddar and return to the oven for another 10–15 minutes or until the cheese is bubbling and golden brown.

Meanwhile, remove the steaks from the fridge at least half an hour before you wish to cook them, shake off any excess marinade and season with salt and pepper.

The steaks can be grilled, barbecued or pan-fried. Either preheat the grill to high, heat a large, non-stick frying pan over a high heat or prepare a barbecue for cooking. Cook the steaks in your chosen way on a fierce heat for 4–5 minutes for rare, 6–7 minutes for medium-rare, or 9–10 minutes for well-done. Allow to rest for 5 minutes on warmed serving plates.

Remove the flavoured butter from the fridge, take it out of the paper wrapper and cut it into slices. Place the butter slices on top of the cooked steaks and add a portion of the potato gratin and some mixed salad to each warmed plate to serve.

Loin of Lamb in Crisp Potato Crust

with Pea & Mint Purée and Tarragon Jus

Serves 4

I've got Lea Linster to thank for this dish. It can be prepared well in advance as, once wrapped in the potato crust, the lamb will sit happily for an hour or two before roasting. Don't be worried by how small the lamb loins appear after being trimmed down – each piece might end up weighing no more than 200g (7oz). The best way to make dried white breadcrumbs for the crust is to toast some bread and simply blitz in a food processor.

Preheat the oven to 200°C (400°F), gas mark 6. Cut the potato into long, thin strips (julienne) using either a mandolin, the coleslaw blade of your food processor, or by hand (see page 28). Pile the strips into the centre of a clean tea towel and squeeze out all of the excess water.

Heat 2 teaspoons of the olive oil in an 18cm (7in) frying pan over a high heat. Reduce the heat a little, sprinkle over half the potato strips in a thin, even layer, and press down the crust as it cooks for about 3–4 minutes until crisp and golden on the bottom, leaving the top of the potato crust uncooked. Slide out of the saucepan crispy-side down, on to a clean tea towel. Repeat with another 2 teaspoons of oil and the remaining potato. Sprinkle the uncooked side of the potato crusts with the parsley.

Place the dried breadcrumbs on a flat plate. Season the trimmed lamb loins well with salt and pepper and then roll each piece in the dried breadcrumbs to evenly coat it all over. Place one loin at the edge of each potato crust. Roll up like a Swiss roll, using the tea towel to lift it up and over, while squeezing the potato tightly around the lamb, so that it sticks to it and completely encloses it.

Use the remaining teaspoon of olive oil to grease a wire rack set in a roasting tin. Transfer the lamb onto the rack, seam-side down (the potato crust stays more crispy that way). Bake for 20–25 minutes for medium or longer if you prefer your meat well-done. »

For the lamb

1 large baking potato, peeled (about 375g/13oz)

5 tsp olive oil

2 tsp chopped flat-leaf parsley

2 tbsp dried white breadcrumbs (see recipe introduction)

2 x 450g (1lb) boneless loins of lamb, completely trimmed of fat

salt and freshly ground black pepper

sprigs of mint, to garnish

For the tarragon jus

50ml (2fl oz) balsamic vinegar

200ml (7fl oz) Madeira Sauce (see page 211)

1 tsp tomato purée

1 tsp light muscovado sugar

1 tbsp chopped tarragon leaves

For the pea and mint purée

4 tbsp double cream

1 tbsp chopped mint

225g (8oz) fresh or frozen peas

1 tbsp butter, at room temperature

2 tbsp milk

Meanwhile, to make the tarragon jus, heat a medium-sized saucepan until quite hot. Add the balsamic vinegar, and as soon as it stops bubbling, add the Madeira Sauce, tomato purée, sugar and tarragon and boil for about 5 minutes until it is reduced by three-quarters and well flavoured. Season with salt and pepper and keep warm over a low heat.

To make the pea purée, place the cream and milk in a medium-sized saucepan with the mint and bring to the boil. Add the peas and butter and cook for 2 minutes (or 4 minutes if the peas are frozen). Season the pea mixture with salt and pepper to taste and then transfer to a food processor. Whiz until well blended to a smooth purée, then pass through a sieve into a clean saucepan and reheat gently. Keep warm over a low heat.

Remove the lamb from the oven and allow to rest, uncovered, on kitchen paper for 5 minutes. Then cut each piece of lamb into four thick slices. Arrange two pieces of lamb on each warmed plate and garnish with fresh mint. Serve with a spoonful of the pea purée alongside and a drizzle of the tarragon jus.

Braised Shoulder
of Lamb
with Champ

Serves 6

Irish lamb really is wonderful. It's at its best in spring and summer, but can still be good later in the year when the lamb available has developed a more mutton-like flavour.

Preheat the oven to 160°C (325°F), gas mark 3. Heat half of the sunflower oil in a large, flameproof casserole, with a lid, over a high heat. Add the lamb and fry for 3–4 minutes until lightly browned on all sides, turning regularly with tongs. Transfer to a plate and set aside. Put the carrots, baby onions and garlic in the casserole and sauté for 5 minutes until lightly golden. Tip into a bowl and set aside.

Return the lamb to the casserole along with the herbs and barley. Pour in the stock and wine and bring to the boil. Season with salt and pepper, cover tightly with foil and then the lid. Cook in the oven for 1½ hours, then remove from the oven, add the reserved vegetables and cook for another hour or until the lamb is very tender and almost falling apart. Carefully lift the lamb out of the dish and allow to cool. Then remove the string, wrap the lamb tightly in foil and place in the fridge for 3–4 hours, or overnight if possible, to help the lamb keep its shape.

Allow the cooking juices to cool completely, then cover and chill until needed. When cool, skim off the solidified fat and strain the liquid from the vegetables through a colander or sieve over a saucepan, setting the vegetables aside. Bring the liquid to the boil, reduce to a simmer and cook for 40–45 minutes until thickened and reduced by half, skimming off any impurities that rise to the surface. Return the vegetables to the sauce and simmer for 5–10 minutes until warmed through. Season with salt and pepper to taste and if the sauce is bitter add the muscovado sugar. Sprinkle with chopped parsley.

Meanwhile, cook the potatoes in a saucepan of boiling salted water for 15–20 minutes or until completely tender. Drain and mash until smooth. Melt the butter in a frying pan over a medium heat. »

2 tbsp sunflower oil
1.8kg (4lb) lamb shoulder, well trimmed, boned and tied (the joint should be about 5cm/2in thick)
200g (7oz) carrots, peeled and cut into wedges
12 baby onions, peeled
4 garlic cloves, peeled and left whole
1 sprig of thyme
2 sprigs of rosemary, plus extra to garnish
50g (2oz) pearl barley, washed
2 litres (3½ pints) beef stock (see page 218)
600ml (1 pint) red wine
1 tsp light muscovado sugar (optional)
1kg (2lb 2oz) floury potatoes, such as Maris Piper, peeled and cut into chunks
75g (3oz) butter
6 spring onions, trimmed and finely sliced
salt and freshly ground black pepper
chopped fresh flat-leaf parsley, to garnish
steamed tenderstem broccoli, to serve

Sauté the spring onions for 2–3 minutes until tender but not browned. Beat the spring onions and butter into the mashed potatoes and season with salt and pepper to taste.

Remove the foil from the cooked lamb and trim off the ends to neaten, then slice the joint into eight pieces, each about 2.5cm (1in) thick. Heat the remaining sunflower oil in a large, non-stick frying pan and very gently sear the lamb slices for 3–4 minutes on each side until golden brown and warmed through. Drain on kitchen paper.

Spoon the champ into warmed, wide-rimmed bowls and arrange two slices of lamb on top of each. Spoon over the vegetables and sauce and serve at once, with the broccoli in a separate serving dish.

Marinated Pork Fillet
with Basil & Pine Nut Stuffing

Serves 4–6

This is based on a recipe that I first cooked at college. I made it again recently and was reminded of just how good it is! The meat really does need to be marinated overnight to achieve the best flavour.

Trim any fat and membrane off the pork and split the fillet lengthways without cutting right through. Open the fillet out flat, cover with cling film and flatten the sides using a mallet, rolling pin or the base of a saucepan, being careful not to put any holes in the meat. Keep the shape as rectangular as possible, with a thickness of no more than 1cm (½in).

Place the garlic, soy sauce, curry powder, ginger, cinnamon, sugar and sunflower oil in a shallow non-metallic dish, large enough to fit the pork fillet comfortably. Stir until well combined, then add the pork to the marinade, and turn to coat. Cover with cling film and chill in the fridge for at least 4 hours, or for up to 24 hours, to allow the flavours to penetrate the meat.

To make the stuffing, place the sausage meat in a food processor with the sweet chilli sauce, basil and egg. Blend until smooth, then slowly add the cream through the feeder tube. »

For the pork

1 x 700g (1½lb) pork fillet (tenderloin)

2 garlic cloves, peeled and crushed

2 tbsp light soy sauce

1 tsp mild curry powder

2 tsp freshly grated root ginger

good pinch of ground cinnamon

1 tbsp light muscovado sugar

2 tbsp sunflower oil

salt and freshly ground black pepper

For the stuffing

200g (7oz) quality sausage meat

2 tbsp sweet chilli sauce

1 tbsp chopped basil, plus sprigs to garnish

1 egg

100ml (3½fl oz) double cream

2 tbsp pine nuts, toasted

buttered noodles and Red Wine Sauce (see page 210), to serve

Season generously with salt and pepper and then blend for another 2 minutes. Transfer to a bowl and mix in the toasted pine nuts, then cover with cling film and chill for at least an hour to firm up.

When ready to cook, preheat the oven to 200°C (400°F), gas mark 6. Remove the marinated pork from the fridge, place on a large sheet of foil and season with salt and pepper. Spread the sausage stuffing thickly in an even layer all over the pork. Using the foil, carefully roll up the pork with the layer of stuffing inside, like a Swiss roll. Twist the ends of the foil tightly and place on a large baking sheet lined with non-stick baking paper. Roast the pork for 50 minutes, turning occasionally until it is cooked through and firm to the touch.

Remove the stuffed pork parcel from the oven and allow it to rest for 5 minutes. Carefully remove the foil and place the pork on a chopping board. Carve on the diagonal into 2.5cm (1in) slices, and arrange on plates on beds of the buttered noodles. Drizzle the Red Wine Sauce around the edge and garnish with basil to serve.

Roast Pork Loin with Roasted Apples

and Sage & Onion Stuffing

Serves 6–8

The combination of pork, apples and sage is a trusted classic! For the best crispy crackling it is important not to baste the rind during cooking. Once the joint is cooked, if the crackling still isn't crispy enough for you, snip it into strips with scissors and flash under the grill. For the roasted apples, do make sure to choose a variety that is in season.

Melt the butter in a large saucepan and gently fry the onion and garlic for 3–4 minutes, stirring occasionally, until softened but not browned, then remove from the heat.

Meanwhile, heat a separate small frying pan over a medium heat and dry fry the pine nuts, tossing a little to ensure they brown evenly.

Stir the breadcrumbs into the onion mixture along with the sage and parsley. Tip in the toasted pine nuts and season with salt and pepper to taste, mixing to combine. Set aside to cool completely.

Preheat the oven to 200°C (400°F), gas mark 6.

Place the pork joint skin-side down on a board and run a sharp knife between the loin and the streaky part to separate them. Continue to cut under the loin part for about 2.5cm (1in), releasing it a little from the fat on the bottom.

Press the cooled stuffing into a large sausage shape and insert it into the opened-up area of the pork joint, pressing it in to fit snugly. Close the opening and roll up the joint, tying it with string at 2.5cm (1in) intervals to secure.

Place the joint, skin-side up, on a rack set in a large roasting tin and pat the skin dry with kitchen paper. Rub the olive oil into the skin with 1 tablespoon of sea salt. Cover with foil and roast for 20 minutes. »

75g (3oz) butter

1 large red onion, peeled and finely chopped

1 garlic clove, peeled and crushed

25g (1oz) pine nuts

125g (4½oz) white breadcrumbs (from a day-old loaf)

2 tsp chopped sage

2 tsp chopped flat-leaf parsley

1.8kg (4lb) boneless pork loin, skin scored at 5mm (¼in) intervals

1 tbsp olive oil

3 eating apples

Maldon sea salt and freshly ground black pepper

Red Wine Sauce, to serve (see page 210)

Reduce the heat to 180°C (350°F), gas mark 4 and roast the joint for another 15 minutes. Then remove the foil and cook for 1¼ hours or until the pork is tender and the crackling is crisp and golden.

When the pork is cooked, transfer it to a warmed serving plate and allow the joint to rest, uncovered, for about 20 minutes. Remove the rack from the roasting tin.

Quarter and core the apples, then cut into slices. Quickly toss the apple slices in the cooking juices and fat left in the roasting tin and return the tin to the oven. Roast the apples for 15–20 minutes until tender and lightly caramelised, tossing once or twice to ensure even cooking.

Cut the string off the rested pork joint and carve the pork into thick slices. Arrange on warmed plates with the roasted apples and drizzle around the Red Wine Sauce to serve.

Roast Pumpkin Risotto
with Rocket Pesto

Serves 4

Pesto isn't just for pasta – it's a great way to flavour risotto, too. If you don't have a mini blender or blender, finely chop the rocket for the pesto, then stir in the Parmesan and olive oil until combined.

Vegetarian

I small pumpkin, peeled, deseeded and cut into 2.5cm (Iin) cubes
8 tbsp olive oil
5 tbsp freshly grated Parmesan cheese
50g (2oz) rocket
1.5 litres (2½ pints) vegetable stock (see page 218)
75g (3oz) unsalted butter
I small onion, peeled and thinly sliced
2 garlic cloves, peeled and crushed
2 tsp chopped sage
350g (12oz) Arborio rice (or other risotto rice)
150ml (¼ pint) dry white wine
50g (2oz) pine nuts, toasted
salt and freshly ground black pepper

Preheat the oven to 200°C (400°F), gas mark 6. Scatter the pumpkin into a roasting tin and drizzle over 2 tablespoons of olive oil. Roast for 40–50 minutes or until tender and golden, tossing occasionally.

To make the rocket pesto, place 1 tablespoon of Parmesan in a mini blender or blender with 4 tablespoons of olive oil and the rocket. Blend briefly to combine – it should retain some texture, and not be too smooth. Season with salt and pepper to taste, transfer to a bowl and cover with cling film, then chill until ready to use.

Pour the stock into a saucepan and bring to a gentle simmer. Heat the remaining olive oil and 50g (2oz) of butter in a separate large saucepan. Add the onion, garlic and sage and cook over a medium heat for 4–5 minutes, stirring occasionally, until soft but not browned. Increase the heat and add the uncooked rice to the pan, cook for 1 minute, stirring continuously until all of the grains are evenly coated with the butter and oil and the rice is opaque. Pour in the wine and allow to reduce for 1–2 minutes, stirring.

Turn down the heat to medium and add a ladleful of stock. Allow to reduce, and stir until completely absorbed. Continue to add the simmering stock, a ladleful at a time, stirring frequently. Allow the stock to be almost completely absorbed before adding the next ladleful. Once all the stock is added the rice should be al dente – just tender but with a slight bite. This should take 20–25 minutes.

Just before serving, stir in the remaining butter and the toasted pine nuts. Carefully fold in the roasted pumpkin, season with salt and pepper and divide among warmed, wide-rimmed bowls. Drizzle with a little rocket pesto (any remaining pesto can be served separately in a small bowl) and top with the rest of the Parmesan cheese.

Wild Mushroom Strudel

Serves 4–6

Vegetarian

2 tbsp olive oil, plus extra for oiling
2 garlic cloves, peeled and crushed
1 small onion, peeled and finely chopped
225g (8oz) mixed wild mushrooms, roughly chopped
2 tbsp double cream
2 tbsp Madeira
1 bunch of spring onions, trimmed and finely chopped
2 tbsp chopped mixed herbs (e.g. basil, parsley and chives)
4–5 sheets filo pastry, thawed if frozen (about 100g/4oz in total)
1 egg, beaten
salt and freshly ground black pepper
mixed salad leaves lightly dressed with French Vinaigrette (see page 220) and warm crusty bread, to serve

This is a wonderful combination of soft mushrooms and crisp pastry. The filo pastry helps to keep the mushroom mixture really moist and full of flavour. The strudel can be prepared several hours in advance as long as it is tightly covered with cling film and kept in the fridge. Then simply pop in the oven once your guests arrive.

Preheat the oven to 190°C (375°F), gas mark 5 and oil a baking sheet.

Heat the olive oil in a large frying pan. Add the garlic, onion and mushrooms and cook over a high heat for 2–3 minutes until almost tender. Reduce the heat, add the cream and Madeira to the pan and cook for another minute. Add the spring onions, herbs and salt and pepper to taste. Sauté for another minute until the spring onions are just tender and the liquid has almost completely reduced. Allow to cool.

Unroll the sheets of filo pastry and place them all, one on top of the other, on a work surface. Brush the top sheet of pastry with beaten egg and then spread over the mushroom mixture to within 4cm (1½in) of the edges. Fold the short ends inwards a little to meet the mushroom mixture and then, starting with a long edge, roll up the pastry fairly tightly like you would a Swiss roll, keeping the mushrooms in place as you roll.

Place the strudel seam-side down on the oiled baking sheet and brush it all over with the remaining beaten egg. Bake for 20–25 minutes until crisp and golden brown.

Allow to cool for a few minutes before sliding off the baking sheet on to a chopping board. Cut the strudel into thick slices and arrange on warmed plates with some dressed mixed salad leaves and crusty bread, if you wish.

Broad Bean & Penne Gratin

with Pecorino

Serves 4–6

Vegetarian

750g (1lb 10oz) fresh or frozen broad beans
350g (12oz) penne pasta
300ml (11fl oz) dry white wine
300ml (11fl oz) double cream
250g (9oz) mascarpone cheese
2 egg yolks
2 tbsp snipped chives
2 tbsp shredded basil leaves
25g (1oz) freshly grated Parmesan cheese
75g (3oz) freshly grated pecorino cheese
salt and freshly ground pepper
mixed salad leaves lightly dressed with French Vinaigrette (see page 220), to serve (optional)

Broad beans add a wonderful flavour to this pasta gratin, while the herby mascarpone cream helps to keep everything really moist. The dish can be prepared several hours in advance and just popped into a preheated oven at 180°C (350°F), gas mark 4 for 25–30 minutes or until it is heated through, then flashed under a hot grill until golden and bubbling.

Place the broad beans in a saucepan of boiling salted water and cook for 2–3 minutes (or about 5 minutes if frozen) until just tender. Drain and refresh the beans under cold running water, then slip them out of their skins.

Meanwhile, cook the pasta in a large saucepan of boiling salted water for 8–10 minutes until al dente (just tender but with a slight bite) or according to the packet instructions. Drain well.

Place the white wine in a small saucepan and heat until it has reduced to about 2 tablespoons. Add the cream and bring to the boil, then season with salt and pepper and turn down the heat. Simmer gently for 6–8 minutes until slightly reduced and thickened. Set aside to cool slightly.

Fold the broad beans and the cream mixture into the cooked penne and tip into a 32 x 18cm (12½ x 7in) ovenproof dish, of 5cm (2in) in depth. Preheat the grill to medium.

Beat together the mascarpone cheese, egg yolks, chives and basil in a bowl with the Parmesan and most of the pecorino, reserving a handful to sprinkle on top. Spoon the mascarpone mixture in dollops over the broad beans and penne and spread using a palette knife or the back of the spoon until the pasta is completely covered. Scatter with the reserved pecorino.

Place the dish under the grill and cook for about 5 minutes until bubbling and lightly golden. Spoon straight from the dish on to warmed plates, with dressed mixed salad leaves, if you wish.

Leek & Mushroom Tart

with Potato Pastry

Serves 4

This tart is made with potato pastry, which is ideal for using up leftover mashed potato and can replace shortcrust pastry for any savoury tart or quiche. Just be careful not to overhandle or it will become tough. If you don't have the exact filling ingredients to hand, feel free to experiment with others.

Vegetarian

100g (4oz) plain flour
75g (3oz) unsalted butter, diced and chilled
100g (4oz) mashed potato
1 tbsp iced water
2 tbsp olive oil
12 small leeks, well trimmed and thinly sliced (about 275g/10oz)
100g (4oz) chestnut mushrooms, wiped and sliced
75g (3oz) mascarpone cheese or 50ml (2fl oz) double cream mixed with 1 egg yolk
50g (2oz) Gorgonzola, dolcelatte or Roquefort cheese, diced
pinch crushed dried chillies (optional)
1 tbsp chopped flat-leaf parsley
salt and freshly ground black pepper
fresh green salad lightly dressed with French Vinaigrette (see page 220), to serve (optional)

Preheat the oven to 200°C (400°F), gas mark 6. To make the potato pastry, sift the flour into a bowl with plenty of salt and pepper. Rub in the butter until the mixture resembles fine breadcrumbs. Mix in the mashed potato, adding a little iced water if necessary, to form a soft dough. Knead the pastry lightly into a ball and then wrap it in cling film. Chill the pastry in the fridge to allow it to firm up for at least 2 hours, or for up to 24 hours.

Heat half the olive oil in a large frying pan and add the leeks. Season with salt and pepper and fry the leeks gently, for about 10 minutes, until well softened but not browned, stirring occasionally. Transfer the leeks to a bowl, then increase the heat and add the remaining olive oil. Tip in the mushrooms, season with salt and pepper and sauté for a few minutes until just tender. Stir the mushrooms into the leeks and set aside to cool.

Sandwich the pastry between two sheets of non-stick baking paper and roll out to a 25cm (10in) circle, about 1cm (½in) thick. Remove the top sheet of paper and slide the bottom one with the pastry on to a baking sheet. Pinch the edges of the pastry to make a rim.

Stir the mascarpone or cream mixture into the leeks and season with salt and pepper to taste, then spoon it over the pastry, spreading the topping out evenly with the back of a spoon. Scatter the blue cheese on top of the tart along with the crushed chillies, if using. Bake for 20–25 minutes or until the pastry rim is golden brown.

Allow to cool for a few minutes, then scatter with parsley and cut into 4–8 wedges. Arrange on warmed plates with salad, if you wish.

Tagliatelle
with Roasted Walnut Pesto

A super-speedy supper dish, this takes just 10 or 15 minutes to prepare, depending on how long your pasta takes to cook. For the pesto, if you don't have a blender, just finely chop the ingredients with a large, sharp knife; or pound in a pestle and mortar. You can use any selection of soft herbs and experiment with different types of nuts. If you wish to make extra pesto, it will keep in the fridge for a couple of days; the colour will fade but it will still taste wonderful. Try it drizzled over bruschetta or grilled fish, or mix with a splash more oil and use as salad dressing.

Serves 4

Vegetarian

12 cherry tomatoes on the vine

5 tbsp olive oil

50g (2oz) walnuts (freshly shelled, if possible)

350g (12oz) tagliatelle

1 garlic clove, peeled and crushed

2 tbsp snipped chives

4 tbsp chopped flat-leaf parsley

4 tbsp freshly grated or shaved Parmesan cheese

salt and freshly ground black pepper

Preheat the oven to 220°C (425°F), gas mark 7. Snip the tomatoes into four bunches, then place in a shallow roasting tin and drizzle over 2 tablespoons of the olive oil. Season generously with salt and pepper and roast for 10–12 minutes or until the tomatoes are starting to brown.

Meanwhile, toast the walnuts in a dry frying pan until lightly golden. Cook the pasta in a large saucepan of boiling salted water for 8–10 minutes until al dente (just tender but with a slight bite) or according to the packet instructions.

Transfer the walnuts and any juices from the tin into a blender or mini blender. Allow to cool with the lid off. Return the tomatoes to the switched-off oven to keep warm. Blitz the walnuts with the remaining olive oil for a few seconds, then add the garlic, herbs and 2 tablespoons of the Parmesan cheese, then pulse briefly until roughly chopped.

Drain the pasta well and return it to the saucepan, then fold in the pesto and season with salt and pepper to taste. Divide the pasta among warmed, wide-rimmed bowls and arrange the roasted tomatoes on the side. Scatter over the remaining Parmesan cheese to serve.

Aubergine & Potato Dhansak

Serves 4–6

This delicious, vegetarian, lentil-based curry can be served with chapattis or pilau rice. If you can't find liquid coconut cream (sold in cartons) use creamed coconut (sold as a solid block) instead. Simply follow the instructions on the packet to make up to the required quantity – it works just as well.

Heat the sunflower oil in a large saucepan over a medium heat and then add the mustard and cumin seeds, cinnamon stick and cloves and allow them to sizzle for 20 seconds. Add the onion, garlic and ginger and cook over a low heat for 10 minutes until softened but not browned, stirring occasionally.

Stir the tomatoes into the onion mixture along with the lentils, potatoes, aubergine, ground coriander, cumin, turmeric, sweet paprika and chilli powder. Pour in the coconut cream and 600ml (1 pint) of the stock, season with salt and pepper and bring slowly to the boil. Reduce the temperature and allow to simmer for 20–25 minutes until the lentils are quite soft and have almost disintegrated into the sauce, and the vegetables are just beginning to soften, stirring occasionally.

Add the cauliflower and the remaining stock, cover and simmer for another 15–20 minutes until the vegetables are tender.

Stir the spinach into the curry mixture and cook for 1–2 minutes until just wilted. Stir in about half of the coriander and ladle into warmed bowls. Top with a dollop of natural yoghurt and sprinkle with the remaining coriander. Serve with plenty of chapattis to soak up all the delicious sauce.

Vegetarian

2 tbsp sunflower oil

2 tsp black mustard seeds

2 tsp cumin seeds

I cinnamon stick

4 whole cloves

I onion, peeled and finely chopped

2 garlic cloves, peeled and crushed

5cm (2in) piece of fresh root ginger, peeled and finely grated

400g tin of chopped tomatoes

75g (3oz) red lentils

225g (8oz) waxy potatoes (e.g. Charlotte), cut into bite-sized pieces

I small aubergine, trimmed and cut into bite-sized pieces

I tbsp each of ground coriander, cumin, turmeric, sweet paprika and chilli powder

200ml carton of coconut cream

900ml (1½ pints) vegetable or chicken stock (see pages 218–19)

275g (10oz) cauliflower, broken into bite-sized florets

75g (3oz) baby spinach leaves

3 tbsp chopped coriander

salt and freshly ground black pepper

natural yoghurt, to garnish

chapattis, to serve

Thai Red Vegetable Curry

with Basil

This curry is quick and easy to prepare, especially now that most supermarkets sell authentic ready-made Thai curry pastes. To adjust for a Thai yellow chicken curry, replace the red curry paste with yellow, add 350g (12oz) chicken strips to the broth and cook for 4 minutes. Then add 100g (4oz) mangetout and a drained 200g (7oz) tin of bamboo shoots and cook for another 3 minutes. Finally, stir in the basil leaves as below.

Heat the sunflower oil in a large saucepan over a medium heat. Add the ginger and garlic and cook gently for about 1 minute without browning, stirring constantly. Add the curry paste and cook, stirring constantly, for a further 2 minutes. Add the coconut milk, sugar, lime juice, soy sauce and stock and bring to the boil. Reduce the heat to a simmer and cook for 2 minutes or until well combined, stirring occasionally.

Stir the butternut squash into the saucepan and simmer for 6 minutes. Add the green beans, sweetcorn and red pepper and simmer for another 5–6 minutes until all the vegetables are tender.

Stir in the basil leaves and remove from the heat. To serve, ladle on to a mound of Thai fragrant rice in warmed, deep bowls.

Serves 4

Vegetarian

2 tbsp sunflower oil

5cm (2in) piece of fresh root ginger, peeled and cut into matchsticks

2 large garlic cloves, peeled and thinly sliced

2 heaped tbsp Thai red curry paste

400g tin of coconut milk

2 tsp light muscovado sugar

juice of 1 lime

2 tbsp light soy sauce or Thai fish sauce (nam pla) for non-vegetarians

300ml (11fl oz) vegetable stock (see page 218)

1 small butternut squash, peeled, deseeded and cut into cubes (about 350g/12oz in total)

100g (4oz) fine green beans, trimmed and halved

100g (4oz) baby sweetcorn, halved lengthways

1 small red pepper, deseeded and cut into strips

15g (½oz) bunch basil, leaves stripped

steamed Thai fragrant rice, to serve

Roasted Vegetable Couscous Salad

with Lemon Hummus Sauce

Serves 4

Vegetarian

2 red peppers, halved, deseeded and cut into 2.5cm (1in) squares

2 yellow peppers, halved, deseeded and cut into 2.5cm (1in) squares

2 large courgettes, trimmed and cut into 2.5cm (1in) pieces

1 large aubergine, trimmed and cut into 2.5cm (1in) pieces

1 large red onion, peeled and cut into 2.5cm (1in) pieces

6 tbsp extra virgin olive oil

handful basil leaves

125g tub of hummus

3 tbsp Greek yoghurt

juice of 1 lemon

225g (8oz) couscous

2 tbsp chopped flat-leaf parsley

Maldon sea salt and freshly ground black pepper

This couscous is delicious hot or cold. Try using any combination of Mediterranean vegetables that you fancy. However, it's important that the vegetables are not too crowded in the roasting tin; otherwise they'll stew rather than roast. If in doubt, use two smaller tins and swap their positions in the oven halfway through roasting to ensure the vegetables cook evenly.

Preheat the oven to 230°C (450°F), gas mark 8. Place a large roasting tin in the oven to heat up.

Place the red and yellow peppers, courgettes, aubergine and onion in a large bowl and drizzle over half of the olive oil, tossing to coat evenly. Tip the vegetables into the heated roasting tin. Season generously with salt and pepper and roast for about 40 minutes or until the vegetables are completely tender and lightly caramelised, tossing from time to time to ensure they cook evenly. About 5 minutes before the vegetables are ready, chop up the basil. Scatter the basil over the vegetables, tossing to combine, then return to the oven to finish cooking.

Place the hummus in a bowl and whisk in the Greek yoghurt, half of the lemon juice and 1 tablespoon of water, then season with salt and pepper to taste. Cover with cling film and chill until needed.

Once you have added the basil to the vegetables, place the couscous in a large saucepan and drizzle over the remaining 3 tablespoons of olive oil with the rest of the lemon juice, stirring gently to combine. Pour over 225ml (8fl oz) of boiling water, then stir well, cover and leave to stand for 5 minutes.

Gently separate the couscous grains with a fork. Season with salt and pepper to taste, then fold in the roasted vegetables and parsley. Serve warm or cold on plates with the hummus sauce drizzled on top.

Fettucine with Melting Courgettes

and Parmesan

Serves 4

This recipe is simple and stunning. Use the smallest courgettes you can find as they have a nuttier flavour and seem to ooze much less water. Look out for dried egg fettucine – it is much lighter in weight than normal pasta so you don't need as much.

Heat the olive oil in a heavy-based frying pan over a low heat. Add the shallots and sauté gently for about 5 minutes until softened but not browned. Add the courgettes, garlic, thyme, chillies and salt and pepper and cook for another 10 minutes until the vegetables are completely softened, stirring occasionally. Increase the heat for the last couple of minutes until the mixture begins to turn golden.

Meanwhile, cook the fettucine in a large saucepan of boiling salted water, stir once and cook for 5 minutes until al dente (just tender but with a slight bite) or according to the packet instructions.

Drain the pasta in a colander and rinse briefly in cold water, draining again. Return the pasta to the saucepan, add the butter and parsley and toss to coat. Stir in the courgette mixture and divide among warmed, wide-rimmed bowls. Add a good grinding of pepper and scatter over the Parmesan cheese. Serve the salad in a separate dish.

Vegetarian

4 tbsp olive oil
2 shallots, peeled and finely chopped
450g (1lb) courgettes, trimmed and cut into 1cm (½in) dice
2 garlic cloves, peeled and finely chopped
2 tsp chopped thyme
½ tsp dried crushed chillies
250g (9oz) dried egg fettucine
25g (1oz) butter
2 tbsp chopped flat-leaf parsley
4 tbsp freshly grated Parmesan cheese
salt and freshly ground black pepper
green salad lightly dressed with French Vinaigrette (see page 220), to serve

Roasted Vegetable Lasagne

Serves 4

This dish is always hugely popular when we put it on the MacNean menu. In summer or autumn, I like to make it with Mediterranean vegetables, particularly when tomatoes are at their best. We make our own pasta, but you can of course use ready-made fresh varieties, widely available to buy.

Preheat the oven to 200°C (400°F), gas mark 6. Place the courgettes, peppers, fennel, red onions and aubergine in a large roasting tin. Drizzle over 3 tablespoons of olive oil, season generously with salt and pepper and roast for 30 minutes or until the vegetables are almost tender and lightly charred. Remove the tin from the oven.

Increase the oven temperature to 220°C (425°F), gas mark 7. Once the oven has reached the higher temperature, stir the tomatoes into the vegetable mixture, then sprinkle over the balsamic vinegar, garlic and chilli. Roast for another 15 minutes until all the vegetables are completely tender and lightly charred.

Bring a large saucepan of water, with a tight-fitting lid, to the boil, add a good pinch of salt and the remaining tablespoon of olive oil. Add the lasagne sheets and cook until al dente (just tender but with a slight bite), then drain well. The drained lasagne needs to be used straight away.

To assemble, place a sheet of lasagne in the middle of each warmed plate and spoon over half of the roasted vegetables, then drizzle a tablespoon of pesto over each one. Repeat with another layer of pasta and cover with the rest of the roasted vegetables, spooning over any remaining juices from the roasting tin. Drizzle over the remaining pesto and then cover with the last sheets of lasagne and garnish with the rocket. Drizzle the Port and Balsamic Syrup around the edge to serve.

Vegetarian

2 courgettes, trimmed and cut into 2.5cm (1in) chunks

1 yellow pepper, quartered, deseeded and cut into chunks

1 red pepper, quartered, deseeded and cut into chunks

1 small fennel bulb, trimmed, quartered and cored

2 red onions, peeled and cut into wedges (keeping roots intact)

1 aubergine, trimmed and cut into chunks

4 tbsp olive oil

3 ripe tomatoes, quartered

1 tbsp balsamic vinegar

3 garlic cloves, peeled and finely chopped

1 red chilli, deseeded and sliced

6 sheets of fresh lasagne, halved across the width

8 tbsp Pesto (see page 208)

salt and freshly ground black pepper

dressed rocket leaves, to garnish

2 tbsp Port and Balsamic Syrup (see page 214), to serve

Desserts
& Petit Fours

Mango & Polenta Upside Down Cake

Serves 8–10

This fabulous cake uses polenta as well as flour, which gives it a very delicate texture. You can use apricots, pears, peaches or pineapple instead of the mango if you prefer, depending on the time of year and what is in season.

Preheat the oven to 200°C (400°F), gas mark 6. Grease a 23cm (9in) loose-bottomed cake tin and lightly dust with flour, knocking out any excess.

Using an electric beater, cream the butter, sugar and vanilla seeds together in a bowl for 5 minutes until lightly and fluffy. Add the two whole eggs, one at a time, beating until smooth after each addition. Add the egg yolks, a little at a time, adding a little flour if the mixture starts to curdle. Beat in the rest of the flour along with the baking powder, cinnamon and polenta until you achieve a smooth batter.

Fan the slices of mango in an even layer in the base of the prepared cake tin and then spoon the cake mixture over the top, spreading it with the back of the spoon until it is smooth and covers the fruit completely. Bake for 20–25 minutes until the top has set and is golden brown, then cover with foil and continue to bake for another 25–30 minutes or until a skewer inserted into the centre comes out clean.

Remove the cake from the oven and allow to cool in the tin for 15–20 minutes. Take the cake out of the tin and invert it on to a flat plate, running a knife between the cake and the tin base to release it without breaking the mango topping.

To serve, cut the mango and polenta cake into slices and arrange on plates. Dollop some cream on the side and decorate with a little dusting of cinnamon.

Ingredients
175g (6oz) butter, softened, plus extra for greasing
100g (4oz) plain flour, plus extra for dusting
200g (7oz) caster sugar
seeds scraped from 1 vanilla pod
2 eggs
4 egg yolks
1 tsp baking powder
½ tsp ground cinnamon, plus extra for sprinkling
75g (3oz) polenta
2 medium ripe mangoes, peeled and sliced into wedges (stone discarded)
whipped cream, to serve

Classic Tarte Tatin
with Cinnamon & Vanilla Syrup

Serves 4–6

Yet another classic French recipe, Tarte Tatin always looks great and tastes fabulous and this one is made with ready-rolled puff pastry for ease. The best way to arrange the apple quarters is to lay them first around the edge of the tin, in a pinwheel fashion. Once a full circle is in place, then fill the space in the middle. It is very important that the apples are tightly packed or they may fall apart during cooking.

You will need a 23–25cm (9–10in) heavy-based, ovenproof frying pan, a Tarte Tatin mould or a shallow, solid cake tin. Unroll the pastry on a clean work surface and carefully cut out a circle, 2.5cm (1in) larger than the frying pan. Place the pastry on a baking sheet lined with non-stick baking paper and chill for at least 30 minutes.

Meanwhile, peel, core and quarter the apples and toss them in half of the lemon juice. Mix the butter in a bowl with the cinnamon and vanilla seeds. Using a spatula, spread the flavoured butter evenly over the base of the frying pan. Sprinkle over the caster sugar in an even layer and then arrange the apple quarters, cut-side up, tightly together in the base of the pan.

Cook over a medium–high heat for about 15 minutes or until the apples are caramelised, cooked through and light golden brown, being careful that they don't catch on the bottom. Remove from the heat, then sprinkle the apples with the lemon zest and the remaining lemon juice. Allow to cool for about 5 minutes, if time allows.

Preheat the oven to 200°C (400°F), gas mark 6. Lay the chilled pastry sheet over the top of the apples, tucking in the edges so that when the tart is turned out, the edges will create a rim that will hold in the caramel and apple juices. Bake for 25–30 minutes until the pastry is crisp and golden brown and the apples are completely tender but still holding their shape. »

Ingredients
225g (8oz) ready-rolled puff pastry, thawed if frozen
750g (1lb 10oz) crisp eating apples (4–5 in total), such as Egremont Russet or Granny Smith
grated zest and juice of 1 large lemon
100g (4oz) unsalted butter, at room temperature
¼ tsp ground cinnamon
seeds scraped from 1 vanilla pod
175g (6oz) golden caster sugar
vanilla ice cream, to serve

Leave the tart in the tin for a minute or two, then loosen the edges with a round-bladed knife if necessary and invert on to a flat plate. Rearrange any apples which have loosened, moving them back into place with a palette knife, and allow to cool for a few minutes. This enables all the juices to be reabsorbed and allows the caramel to set a little. Cut into slices and serve on slightly warmed plates with scoops of vanilla ice cream.

Cheat's Banoffee Pie
with Chocolate Drizzle

Serves 6

You can buy jars of toffee sauce in most major supermarkets, so don't worry about making your own. The base needs at least 15 minutes to set and the topping is best left for an hour. However, if you're in a real hurry don't bother with the chocolate drizzle, simply crumble a chocolate flake on top instead.

250g (9oz) digestive biscuits

vegetable oil, for oiling

150g (5oz) butter

350g jar of toffee sauce

2 large ripe bananas

300ml (11fl oz) double cream

25g (1oz) plain or milk chocolate, broken into squares

Place the biscuits in a plastic bag, seal the bag and crush the biscuits into fine crumbs using a rolling pin. Lightly oil a 23cm (9in) round, loose-bottomed, fluted flan tin, of 4cm (1½in) in depth.

Melt the butter in a medium-sized saucepan over a medium heat, then remove from the heat and stir in the crushed biscuits. Press the mixture into the base and up the sides of the oiled flan tin. Chill for at least 15 minutes or for up to 24 hours.

Peel and thinly slice the bananas. Spread the toffee sauce over the set biscuit base and cover with the sliced bananas. Lightly whip the cream in a bowl until soft peaks form. Spoon the cream on top of the bananas and spread it out, right to the edge of the biscuit base, so that the banana slices are completely covered. Swirl the top attractively and chill for at least an hour.

When ready to serve, melt the chocolate in a heatproof bowl set over a saucepan of simmering water or in the microwave. Leave to cool to room temperature, then drizzle over the cream topping. Carefully remove the pie from the flan tin and cut into slices to serve.

Warm Pear Tarts

with Butterscotch Sauce

Serves 6

Look out for authentic Greek filo pastry for these tarts. If you can, buy it in a 275g packet, which is the perfect amount for the recipe. To prevent the pastry drying out, cover with a clean, damp tea towel while not in use. Individual tarts always look impressive; however, you can also make this as one larger tart, using a 23cm (9in) loose-bottomed tart tin, of 2.5cm (1in) in depth. Leave the filo sheets whole as you brush them with butter and layer up as described below. Arrange the pears over the frangipane with the narrow ends angled towards the centre and bake for 40–45 minutes.

To prepare the pears, place the apple juice in a medium-sized saucepan with the sugar, cinnamon stick, halved vanilla pod and star anise. Bring to the boil, then reduce the heat and add the pears. Simmer gently for 10–15 minutes until the pears are tender but still holding their shape.

Remove the saucepan from the heat and allow the pears to cool completely in the syrup. Once they are cool, carefully lift them out and drain briefly on kitchen paper. Discard the cinnamon stick, vanilla pod and star anise and reserve the liquid in the saucepan.

Meanwhile, make the frangipane filling. Place the butter and icing sugar in a large bowl. Using a hand-held beater, whisk them together until they are light and fluffy. Beat in the flour and ground almonds, then gradually beat in the eggs, vanilla seeds and cinnamon. Beat well until the mixture has a thick, smooth consistency.

Preheat the oven to 190°C (375°F), gas mark 5. Melt the unsalted butter in a small saucepan or in the microwave, then remove from the heat and allow to cool.

Unfold the filo pastry and cut the sheets into quarters, then cover with a clean, damp tea towel. Take a piece of the filo and brush it with some melted butter. Add another three layers of the brushed filo pastry, placing each square at a slightly different angle. »

For the pears and pastry

600ml (1 pint) apple juice

50g (2oz) caster sugar

1 cinnamon stick

½ split vanilla pod

2 whole star anise

3 ripe small pears, peeled, halved and cored (use a melon baller if you have one)

75g (3oz) unsalted butter

6 filo pastry sheets (see recipe introduction), thawed if frozen

25g (1oz) flaked almonds

vanilla ice cream, to serve

For the frangipane filling

100g (4oz) butter, at room temperature

100g (4oz) icing sugar

25g (1oz) plain flour

100g (4oz) ground almonds

2 eggs, beaten

seeds scraped from ½ vanilla pod

¼ tsp ground cinnamon

For the butterscotch sauce

100ml (3½fl oz) double cream

25g (1oz) butter, diced

2 tbsp dark rum

Repeat until you have six piles of layered up pieces of filo. Lift each pile of filo and use it to line a 10cm (4in) round tartlet tin, of 2cm (¾in) in depth, pressing down the corners and scrunching the excess into the curved sides of each tin.

Divide the frangipane filling between the filo-lined tartlet tins, spreading it evenly with the back of a spoon. Arrange half a pear on top of each one, cut side down, pressing it down slightly into the mixture. Sprinkle with the flaked almonds and bake for 20–25 minutes until firm to the touch and golden. Check that the tarts are cooked through by piercing one with a skewer at an angle through the middle; if it comes out clean, the tarts are ready.

Meanwhile, make the butterscotch sauce. Bring to the boil the reserved liquid from poaching the pears, then turn down the heat and simmer for 15–20 minutes until reduced by a quarter and syrupy. Add the cream, diced butter and rum, stirring until combined, and then simmer gently for another 5 minutes until thickened. Allow to cool for 10–15 minutes until thickened a little further.

To serve, carefully remove the warm pear tarts from the tartlet tins and arrange on plates. Spoon the butterscotch sauce alongside and serve at once with vanilla ice cream.

Passion fruit Panna Cotta

with Poached Autumn Berries

Panna cotta is a set Italian cream that is a cross between a mousse and a crème brûlée (but without the crunchy topping). What makes this version a little different is the addition of coconut milk, which gives them a truly exotic flavour. The thin layer of passion fruit jelly on the top makes them look really stunning.

To make the panna cotta, put the gelatine leaves in a bowl of cold water and leave to soak for 10 minutes. Put the cream, coconut milk, sugar and scraped-out vanilla seeds into a small saucepan and slowly bring to the boil. Take the saucepan off the heat, gently squeeze the soaked gelatine leaves dry and add them to the pan, whisking continuously until they have dissolved. Strain the mixture through a sieve into a measuring jug. Allow to cool completely – this will take about 1½ hours.

To make the passion fruit jelly, place the gelatine leaves in a small bowl and pour over enough cold water to cover. Set aside for 10 minutes, then squeeze out the excess water. Place the orange juice, passion fruit seeds and sugar in a saucepan. Bring to the boil and then stir in the squeezed-out gelatine. Stir well to combine and then allow to cool a little. Strain through a fine sieve.

Divide the cooled passion fruit jelly between six 150ml (¼ pint) dariole moulds or ramekins. Place on a baking sheet, cover with cling film and leave to set in the fridge for at least 1 hour.

Once the panna cotta mixture is cool, give it a good stir to disperse the vanilla seeds, then divide the mixture equally between the moulds and leave them to set again in the fridge for at least 3 hours, or for up to 2 days.

Meanwhile, prepare the poached berries. Place the red wine, crème de cassis, sugar, cinnamon, star anise and vanilla seeds in a small saucepan with a lid. »

For the panna cotta mixture

4 gelatine leaves

500ml (18fl oz) double cream

100ml (3½fl oz) coconut milk

100g (4oz) caster sugar

seeds scraped from 1 vanilla pod

For the passion fruit jelly

2 gelatine leaves

150ml (¼ pint) freshly squeezed orange juice

3 passion fruits, cut in half and seeds removed

25g (1oz) caster sugar

For the poached berries

3 tbsp red wine

2 tbsp crème de cassis

50g (2oz) caster sugar

1 cinnamon stick

1 whole star anise

seeds scraped from ½ vanilla pod

¼ tsp freshly grated root ginger

100g (4oz) mixed autumn berries (such as blackberries, blueberries, tayberries and redcurrants)

mint sprigs, to decorate

Stir in 50ml (2fl oz) of cold water and bring to the boil. Turn down the heat and simmer for 10–15 minutes until well reduced and syrup-like. Stir in the ginger and berries. Cover the pan with the lid, remove from the heat and allow the berries and syrup to cool completely. This should take about an hour.

To serve, unmould the panna cotta by dipping very briefly into hot water, then place a plate face down on top of each mould and invert, allowing them to drop out on their own. Spoon some poached fruits around the edge and decorate with the mint sprigs to serve.

Pineapple Carpaccio
with Mint and Passion fruit

Serves 4–6

50g (2oz) caster sugar
finely grated zest and juice of 1 lime
2 passion fruits
½ small mild red chilli, deseeded and finely shredded
1 large ripe pineapple
2 tbsp finely shredded mint leaves
passion fruit or mango sorbet, to serve (optional)

For the very best results, leave the carpaccio at room temperature for a couple of hours before serving to allow the syrup flavours to infuse the pineapple. Just make sure you don't add the mint to the syrup before it has cooled down or it will turn black and the end result will not look as pretty.

Pour 120ml (4½fl oz) of water into a small, heavy-based saucepan. Add the sugar and lime juice and bring to a gentle simmer for 2–3 minutes, stirring until the sugar has dissolved. Remove from the heat. Cut the passion fruits in half and scoop out the seeds, then stir into the sugar syrup. Stir in the chilli and allow to cool.

Meanwhile, slice the top and bottom off the pineapple, sit it upright on a board and slice away the skin and all the little brown 'eyes'. Using an apple corer, remove the core and then, using a very sharp knife, slice the pineapple as thinly as possible. Cover the base of a platter or individual plates with the slices and set aside.

When the sugar syrup has cooled, stir in the lime zest and mint and drizzle over the pineapple carpaccio. Cover with cling film and set aside at room temperature for 2 hours if time allows. Remove the cling film and serve on individual plates with scoops of passion fruit sorbet, if you wish.

Amaretti Baked Peaches
with Mascarpone Cream

Italian Amaretti biscuits are delicious crumbled on to soft fruit. Of course, you can use nectarines for this recipe or even drained canned peaches if there are none in season. Buy the ones in natural fruit juice as they aren't too sweet.

Preheat the oven to 180°C (350°F), gas mark 4. Place the peaches in a heatproof bowl and pour over enough boiling water to cover. Set aside for 1 minute, then drain and cover with cold water. Cut each one in half, then remove the stones and peel the skin away.

Place the Amaretti biscuits into a plastic bag, seal and crush with a rolling pin into fine crumbs. Tip into a bowl and mix in the sugar, vanilla extract, egg yolks and lemon juice.

Grease a shallow ovenproof dish. Arrange the peach halves in the dish and fill the holes in the middle with the Amaretti mixture. Bake for 20–25 minutes until the filling is golden and the peaches are completely tender but still holding their shape.

Meanwhile, mix the mascarpone in a bowl with the sugar and vanilla extract, then add the cream and whisk until smooth and just holding its shape.

Remove the peaches from the oven and allow to cool slightly, then transfer to plates and add a dollop of the mascarpone cream to the side.

For the peaches

4–6 large ripe peaches

75g (3oz) Amaretti biscuits

1 tbsp caster sugar

few drops of vanilla extract

2 egg yolks

2 tsp fresh lemon juice

butter, for greasing

For the mascarpone cream

100g (4oz) mascarpone cheese

2 tsp caster sugar

few drops of vanilla extract

100ml (4fl oz) double cream

Warm Raspberry Shortcake

with Balsamic Syrup

This recipe was given to me by my good friend Neil McFadden. The shortbread discs can be made up to 24 hours in advance, then stored in an airtight container until ready to use. The pastry cream will also keep in the fridge for a week or you can freeze it, making this a great dessert to prepare well in advance.

To make the shortbread, place the butter and icing sugar in a bowl and then sift the flour, cornflour and salt on top. Using a hand-held beater, beat until you have achieved a smooth dough, adding a tablespoon of cold water to help bring the mixture together if necessary. Cover with cling film. Place in the fridge to rest for at least 1 hour and preferably overnight.

Line two baking sheets with non-stick baking paper. Roll out the shortbread on a lightly floured work surface to a thickness of 3mm (⅛in). Cut out 18 discs using a 7.5cm (3in) fluted cutter and place them on the lined baking sheets. Allow to rest again in the fridge for 20 minutes, this will help prevent them shrinking during cooking.

Preheat the oven to 180°C (350°F), gas mark 4. Bake the shortbread rounds for 8–10 minutes or until they are lightly golden. Using a fish slice, transfer them to a wire rack to cool.

To make the pastry cream, place the milk in a small saucepan with the vanilla seeds. Bring to the boil and remove from the heat.

Using a hand-held beater, beat the egg yolks in a bowl with the sugar and flour, until pale and thick enough that when you swirl the beaters in a figure-of-eight pattern, they leave a trail. Remove the vanilla pod from the milk and carefully pour the heated milk on to the egg yolk mixture, stirring to combine. Transfer the mixture to a clean saucepan and cook over a very low heat for 2–3 minutes, stirring continuously, until very thick. Do not allow the mixture to boil or it will curdle. **»**

For the shortbread

150g (5oz) butter, diced, at room temperature, plus extra for greasing

75g (3oz) icing sugar, plus extra to decorate

150g (5oz) plain flour, plus extra for dusting

75g (3oz) cornflour

pinch of salt

For the pastry cream

150ml (¼ pint) milk

seeds scraped from ½ vanilla pod

2 egg yolks

25g (1oz) caster sugar

1 tbsp plain flour

For the balsamic syrup

50g (2oz) caster sugar

1 tbsp balsamic vinegar

seeds scraped from ½ vanilla pod

To assemble

275g (10oz) raspberries

mint sprigs, to decorate

vanilla ice cream, to serve

Pour into a clean bowl and place a piece of cling film on the surface to prevent a skin forming. Allow to cool completely, then chill until needed.

To make the balsamic syrup, place the sugar in a heavy-based saucepan with 2 tablespoons of water and bring to the boil, then reduce the heat and simmer for 10–15 minutes until you have achieved a rich, golden caramel colour. Quickly and carefully stir in the balsamic vinegar (stand back as it will splutter) and add another 100ml (3½fl oz) of cold water, along with the vanilla seeds. The sugar will seize up and harden but simply increase the heat and stir to dissolve. Simmer for 2–3 minutes until you have a slightly thickened syrup. Set aside to cool completely and thicken further.

Now assemble the shortcakes. Set aside some of the raspberries to use later for decoration. Place one of the shortbread discs on a baking sheet lined with non-stick baking paper, spoon a tablespoon of pastry cream into the centre and arrange some raspberries around the edge. Top with another shortbread disc and repeat the cream and raspberry layer. Finish with a third shortbread disc and dust liberally with icing sugar. Repeat with the remaining ingredients to make six shortcake stacks in total. Place in the oven for 3–4 minutes at 180°C (350°F), gas mark 4 to just warm through.

Arrange the warm raspberry shortcake stacks on plates and decorate the tops with the mint sprigs and the reserved raspberries. Drizzle the Balsamic Syrup around the edge, stirring in a few drops of boiling water to loosen if necessary, and add a scoop of ice cream to each plate to serve.

Lemon & Mascarpone Mousse

Serves 8

This creamy, zesty dessert is delicious on its own, or you can make it even more special by serving it with roasted apricots, fresh summer berries or poached rhubarb, depending on the time of year and what fruit is in season.

5 gelatine leaves
300ml (11fl oz) milk
1 lemongrass stalk, outer layers removed and finely sliced
3 egg yolks
75g (3oz) caster sugar
seeds scraped from 1 vanilla pod
finely grated zest and juice of 2 lemons
250g tub mascarpone cheese, at room temperature
300ml (11fl oz) double cream
mint sprigs, to decorate

Place the gelatine leaves in a small bowl and pour over enough cold water to cover. Set aside for 10 minutes.

Place the milk and lemongrass in a saucepan. Bring to the boil and then remove from the heat.

Using an electric beater, whisk the egg yolks in a bowl with the caster sugar and vanilla seeds until pale and thickened. Remove the lemongrass stalk from the hot milk and gradually pour the milk into the egg mixture, whisking continuously until evenly mixed.

Pour the custard back into a clean saucepan and cook over a low heat until the mixture coats the back of a wooden spoon, stirring continuously. Do not allow the mixture to boil or it will curdle.

Pass the custard through a fine sieve into a large bowl. Drain the gelatine leaves and squeeze out the excess liquid, then stir the leaves into the custard until dissolved. Add the lemon zest and juice, stirring to combine. Set the bowl in another, larger bowl half filled with ice and set aside for 1½ hours until the mousse is just beginning to set and hold its shape.

Once the custard has set, whisk the mascarpone in a bowl until smooth. Whip the cream in a separate bowl until it forms soft peaks and fold into the set custard along with the whisked mascarpone. Pour into eight 150ml (¼ pint) dariole moulds or ramekins, arrange on a baking tray, cover with cling film and place in the fridge for at least 2 hours to set. These can be left in the fridge for up to 2 days.

Arrange the ramekins on plates and decorate the mousses with mint sprigs to serve.

Cointreau-infused Strawberry Meringues

Serves 6

These meringues have a crisp exterior and delicious, marshmallow centres. They will keep for at least a week in an airtight container, but don't add the strawberry topping until just before serving or the meringues will go soft.

Preheat the oven to 140°C (275°F), gas mark 1. Place the egg whites in a large bowl with the salt and whisk with a hand-held electric beater until they form stiff peaks. Whisk in the sugar, a tablespoon at a time, to make a stiff glossy meringue. Whisk in the cornflour and vinegar.

Drop six even-sized spoonfuls of the meringue mixture on to a large baking sheet lined with non-stick baking paper, spacing them well apart. Flatten the meringues slightly with the back of a metal spoon, making a small dip in the centre. Bake the meringues for 45 minutes.

Turn off the oven but leave the meringues inside for 2–3 hours to go completely cold. This should stop them from cracking.

Half an hour before serving, prepare the topping. Place the strawberries in a bowl and gently mix with the icing sugar, orange zest and Cointreau. Set aside to allow the flavours to infuse.

Just before serving, whip the cream in a large bowl until it forms soft peaks. Spoon a small dollop of the cream in the centre of each plate and sit the meringues on top to prevent them from sliding around on the plates. Spoon the whipped cream on top. Pile the strawberries on top, drizzling any juices around the plates, and serve.

For the meringues

3 egg whites

pinch of salt

175g (6oz) caster sugar

1 tsp cornflour

½ tsp white wine vinegar

For the topping

225g (8oz) small ripe strawberries, hulled and halved

1 tbsp sifted icing sugar

¼ tsp finely grated orange zest

1 tbsp Cointreau (or other orange-flavoured liqueur)

300ml (11fl oz) double cream

Chocolate Fondants
with Poached Cherries

Serves 10

These can be made well in advance as they are better if allowed to rest for a few hours before baking. Once cooked, they should be soft in the centre, but able to hold their shape. If they collapse, simply cook for a few more minutes. Any extra fondants can be frozen for up to 1 month and the poached cherries will keep for a week in the fridge.

To poach the cherries, place the wine in a saucepan with the kirsch, if using, sugar, cinnamon and vanilla pod and bring to the boil. Turn down the heat and simmer for 10 minutes until the flavours have combined and the liquid has slightly reduced. Add the cherries and simmer for 5 minutes until they are soft and tender but still holding their shape. Remove from the heat, stir well and allow to cool. Cover with cling film until needed.

Meanwhile, thoroughly grease ten 175ml (6fl oz) dariole moulds or ramekins with butter and then dust with plain flour. Place in the freezer to set for at least 10 minutes.

To make the fondants, melt the butter and chocolate in a heatproof bowl set over a saucepan of simmering water. Remove from the heat and allow to cool a little. Whisk the eggs, egg yolks and sugar in a large bowl until light and fluffy. Beat the chocolate mixture into the egg mixture, then gently fold in the flour.

Pipe or spoon the chocolate mixture into the prepared moulds until each is no more than about a third full, gently tapping to remove any air bubbles. Place three chocolate drops into the centre of each mould, then add the remaining chocolate mixture until the chocolate drops are completely covered but the dariole moulds are no more than half full. Place the moulds in the fridge for at least 15 minutes (or for up to 3 hours) until the mixture is firm but still a little sticky to the touch.

Preheat the oven to 190°C (375°F), gas mark 5. Bake the fondants for 12 minutes until they are just cooked but still soft in the centre. »

For the poached cherries

300ml (11fl oz) red wine

2 tbsp kirsch (cherry brandy), optional

500g (1lb 2oz) cherries, stones removed (use a melon baller if you have one) and stalks intact

75g (3oz) caster sugar

1 cinnamon stick

½ vanilla pod

For the fondants

200g (7oz) butter, plus a little extra for greasing

100g (4oz) plain flour, sifted, plus a little extra for dusting

200g (7oz) plain chocolate (minimum 70% cocoa solids), broken into squares

4 eggs

4 egg yolks

250g (9oz) caster sugar

30 plain chocolate drops

vanilla ice cream and sprigs of mint, to serve

Allow the fondants to rest for a minute or two in the moulds, then invert each one on to the middle of a plate. Spoon some of the poached cherries alongside, add a scoop of ice cream to each plate and decorate with sprigs of mint.

Mulled Fruit Trifle

Serves 6

My mum always used to make this trifle for special occasions when I was growing up. I loved to help her (especially when it came to clearing up the leftovers!) and it definitely helped inspire me to become a chef. At Christmas I like to decorate the top of this trifle with pomegranate seeds to make it sparkle!

To make the custard, place the milk, cream, and scraped vanilla pod in a medium-sized, heavy-based saucepan over a gentle heat and cook until nearly boiling – but don't allow to boil. Meanwhile, place the egg yolks, sugar, cornflour and vanilla seeds in a large bowl and whisk together until pale and thickened.

Remove the milk and cream mixture from the heat, discard the vanilla pod and slowly whisk into the egg mixture until smooth. Pour back into the saucepan, place on a gentle heat and cook without boiling, stirring continuously, until it coats the back of a wooden spoon. Remove the pan from the heat, cover the custard with a piece of cling film to prevent a skin forming on top and allow to cool.

Meanwhile, prepare the mulled fruit. Place the port in a large saucepan with the sugar, mixed spice and vanilla seeds and bring to the boil. Reduce the heat and simmer for 4–5 minutes until syrupy, stirring occasionally. Stir in the frozen fruits and set aside until cooled, stirring gently from time to time. The fruits should thaw naturally in the hot syrup but still hold their shape.

Place the mulled fruits in the base of a 1.5 litre (2½ pint) glass serving bowl. Scatter over the Madeira sponge and top with the cooled custard. Chill for at least 1 hour until the custard sets a little firmer, or for up to 24 hours. When ready to serve, whip the cream in a mixing bowl until it forms soft peaks and place spoonfuls on top of the custard, gently spreading it with a palette knife or the back of a metal spoon to cover the custard completely. Sprinkle with the toasted flaked almonds.

For the custard

100ml (11fl oz) milk

100ml (3½fl oz) double cream

seeds scraped from ½ vanilla pod, pod also retained

5 egg yolks

4 tbsp caster sugar

2 tsp cornflour

For the mulled fruit

100ml (3½fl oz) ruby red port

100g (4oz) caster sugar

1 tsp ground mixed spice

seeds scraped from ½ vanilla pod

500g bag of frozen fruits of the forest

For the rest of the trifle

200g (7oz) Madeira cake, broken into pieces

300ml (11fl oz) double cream

toasted flaked almonds, to decorate

Nutella Cheesecake

Serves 6–8

This decadent cheesecake is fabulously smooth, silky and rich. It is perfect for keeping in the fridge and helping yourself to whenever you're tempted. If you want to increase the chocolate hit, try using chocolate ginger nut biscuits for the base.

Preheat the oven to 160°C (325°F), gas mark 3. Lightly grease a 23cm (9in) springform cake tin.

Melt the butter in a saucepan over a gentle heat or in a heatproof bowl in the microwave. Add the crushed ginger nut biscuits and mix well. Spread the mixture evenly over the base of the greased tin, pressing down with the back of a spoon to flatten. Place in the fridge to chill for 15 minutes.

Fill an ovenproof dish or roasting tin with hot water and place on the bottom shelf of the oven – this will stop a skin from forming on the cheesecake during cooking. Place the vanilla seeds, mascarpone cheese, sugar, cornflour, eggs, Nutella and stem ginger in a food processor bowl and use the paddle attachment to beat until smooth, or use a hand-held blender.

Pour this mixture on to the biscuit base in the cake tin and place the tin on a baking sheet. Bake for 50–55 minutes until the cheesecake is just set around the edges but still a little wobbly in the centre. Turn off the oven, open the door and carefully run a knife around the edge of the cake tin – this prevents the cheesecake from splitting in the middle while cooling. Close the oven door and leave the cheesecake in the oven for 1½ hours until it is completely set. Remove from the oven and place in the fridge if not serving immediately.

To serve, transfer the cheesecake to a cake stand and cut into wedges in front of your guests. Add a dollop of whipped cream to each plate.

For the base

75g (3oz) butter, plus extra for greasing

250g (9oz) ginger nut biscuits, crushed

For the filling

seeds scraped from 1 vanilla pod

2 x 250g tubs mascarpone cheese

100g (4oz) caster sugar

2 tbsp cornflour

3 eggs

200g jar of Nutella (or other chocolate and hazelnut spread)

1 tsp finely chopped stem ginger

whipped cream, to serve

White Chocolate Tiramisu

Serves 8

For a sophisticated touch, I like to serve this dessert in martini glasses, but you can always just layer it up in one large glass serving dish if you prefer. Mascarpone is a rich, creamy cheese originating from Lodi in the Lombardy region of Italy. It has a sweetened taste and is a classic ingredient in tiramisu.

To make the custard, place the egg yolks in a large bowl with the cornflour, sugar and vanilla seeds. Whisk with an electric beater for a few minutes until pale and thickened. Place the milk and cream in a medium-sized saucepan and bring to the boil, then immediately remove from the heat. Gradually whisk the hot milk and cream into the egg mixture until smooth, then pour back into the pan and place over a gentle heat. Cook gently for about 6–8 minutes on a medium heat, stirring constantly, until the custard coats the back of a wooden spoon. Transfer to a large bowl and allow to cool a little.

Meanwhile, place 2 tablespoons of the double cream in a small saucepan with half of the white chocolate and stir over a low heat for 1–2 minutes until smooth. Remove from the heat and whisk into the cooled custard. Allow to cool completely, then place a fresh piece of cling film on the surface, again to prevent a skin from forming.

To poach the raspberries, place the red wine in a medium-sized saucepan with the sugar, cinnamon stick and vanilla seeds and pod and bring to the boil. Turn down the heat and simmer for 15 minutes until reduced by half and slightly thickened. Place the raspberries in a heatproof bowl and pour the wine mixture over them through a fine sieve, discarding the cinnamon stick and vanilla pod. Stir to combine and allow to cool. »

For the custard

5 egg yolks

1 tbsp cornflour

3 tbsp caster sugar

seeds scraped from ½ vanilla pod

300ml (11fl oz) milk

100ml (3½fl oz) double cream

For the poached raspberries

300ml (11fl oz) red wine

75g (3oz) caster sugar

1 cinnamon stick

seeds scraped from ½ vanilla pod, pod also retained

350g (12oz) raspberries, plus extra to decorate

cocoa powder and sprigs of mint, to decorate

For the rest of the tiramisu

150ml (¼ pint) double cream

175g (6oz) white chocolate, grated

500g (1lb 2oz) mascarpone cheese, at room temperature

16 sponge fingers

Whip the remaining cream in a bowl until it forms soft peaks. When the custard is cold, whisk in the mascarpone cheese until completely smooth and then fold in the remaining grated white chocolate and the whipped cream until evenly mixed.

Spoon the poached raspberries, reserving the liquid, into the base of eight 200ml (7fl oz) martini glasses, then arrange two sponge fingers in each glass, breaking them up as necessary to fit. Pour the raspberry liquid over and then spoon the white chocolate mixture on top to cover completely. Chill for 1 hour until set.

Dust each white chocolate tiramisu liberally with cocoa powder and serve decorated with the extra raspberries and sprigs of mint.

Coconut Crème Brûlée
with Spun Sugar Curls

Serves 8

I use a blowtorch to melt and glaze the brûlée sugar topping until it caramelises, but blowtorches are not for the faint-hearted! Instead, you can place the brûlées under a hot grill, but watch them like a hawk because they burn easily. When glazed, they should be a nice mahogany brown colour. The spun sugar curls are a lovely finishing touch, but feel free to leave them out if you're nervous or short on time. Powdered glucose is available from most chemists.

Preheat the oven to 150°C (300°F), gas mark 2. Place the egg yolks in a large bowl with 125g (4½oz) of the sugar and the vanilla seeds. Whisk for about 5 minutes until pale and fluffy – if you swirl the whisk through the mixture in a figure-of-eight shape, the mixture should hold the trail.

Meanwhile, place the milk in a small saucepan with the cream, coconut milk and vanilla pod and simmer gently until the mixture just comes to the boil. Remove the vanilla pod and slowly pour the hot coconut milk into the yolk mixture, whisking continuously. Pour the mixture through a sieve into a clean bowl. »

For the crème brûlée

8 egg yolks
250g (9oz) caster sugar
seeds scraped from I vanilla pod, pod also retained
300ml (11fl oz) milk
600ml (1 pint) double cream
400g tin of coconut milk

For the spun sugar

225g (8oz) caster sugar
I tbsp powdered glucose

Place six 200ml (7fl oz) ramekins in a baking tin filled with enough boiling water to come halfway up the sides of the ramekins. This is called a 'bain marie'. Using a ladle, divide the mixture between the ramekins and then cover the tin tightly with foil. Bake in the oven for 50–55 minutes until just set but still with a slight wobble in the middle.

Remove from the oven and leave in the bain marie, still covered with foil, for another 30 minutes before removing and allowing to cool completely. Transfer to the fridge and allow to set for at least 6 hours or preferably overnight.

About half an hour before serving, place the sugar, glucose and 250ml (9fl oz) of water into a small, heavy-based saucepan. Bring to the boil and then reduce the heat and simmer for 15–20 minutes until the mixture turns a golden caramel colour. The sugar syrup should have a thick honey consistency and should not be too runny. It will thicken a little as it cools, but if it gets too thick, simply heat again and it will quickly loosen.

Using a small, clean, metal spoon and a knife-sharpening steel, dip the spoon into the caramel and lift it out again, then twist it around the steel to create some sugar curls, working very carefully as the caramel will be extremely hot. Remove the curls from the steel once they are cool and hardened.

Sprinkle the remaining caster sugar over the brûlées in an even layer, and use a blowtorch to melt and glaze the sugar until it caramelises. Place the ramekins on plates to serve and decorate with the spun sugar curls.

Chocolate Brownie
with Fudge Sauce and Caramelised Pecans

Serves 8–10

These intensely chocolatey brownies get smothered in a rich fudge sauce that is flavoured with – you've guessed it – more chocolate! If the brownies have gone cold and you want to heat them up in a hurry, pour over some of the fudge sauce and flash under a hot grill until bubbling.

Preheat the oven to 170°C (325°F), gas mark 3. Line a 30 x 25cm (12 x 10in) baking tin, 5cm (2in) deep, with non-stick baking paper.

For the caramelised pecans, place 25g (1oz) of the butter and 25g (1oz) of the sugar in a small, heavy-based saucepan along with the pecan nuts. Cook over a low heat for 4–5 minutes until the pecan nuts are lightly toasted and caramelised. Spread out on a baking sheet lined with non-stick baking paper and allow to cool before breaking up a little.

Place 100g (4oz) of the chopped chocolate in a heatproof bowl with the remaining butter and set over a saucepan of simmering water until melted, then stir to combine. Remove from the heat and allow to cool a little.

Meanwhile, whisk the eggs in a bowl until stiff, then whisk in the remaining sugar until you have achieved a stiff sabayon. It should hold a trail when the whisk is swirled in a figure-of-eight motion. Sift the flour and cocoa powder into the sabayon and gently fold in. Add the cooled, melted chocolate mixture, the remaining finely chopped chocolate and the caramelised pecan nuts. Continue folding gently until all the ingredients are just about combined.

Pour the chocolate mixture into the lined tin. Bake for 20 minutes and then turn the tin around and bake for another 10 minutes until the top is crusty but the centre is still a little soft. »

For the brownies and pecans

225g (8oz) butter

275g (10oz) caster sugar

100g (4oz) pecan nuts, roughly chopped

275g (10oz) plain chocolate (minimum 70% cocoa solids), finely chopped

4 eggs

100g (4oz) self-raising flour

75g (3oz) cocoa powder

vanilla ice cream or softly whipped cream, to serve

For the fudge sauce

150ml (¼ pint) double cream

25g (1oz) caster sugar

25g (1oz) butter

175g (6oz) plain chocolate (minimum 70% cocoa solids), finely chopped

If intending to serve the brownies warm, begin making the fudge sauce about 10 minutes before the end of the brownie cooking time. Place the cream in a medium-sized saucepan with the sugar and butter and bring to the boil, stirring. Reduce the heat and simmer gently for 4–5 minutes until thickened and becoming syrupy, stirring occasionally to prevent the mixture from catching on the base of the pan. Remove from the heat and allow to cool a little.

Meanwhile, melt the chocolate for the sauce in a heatproof bowl set over a saucepan of simmering water. Whisk into the fudge sauce until smooth and well combined. Serve warm or transfer to a bowl and allow to cool completely, then cover with cling film and keep in the fridge until needed. The sauce will keep for up to 1 week.

Remove the brownies from the oven and allow to cool slightly before lifting out of the tin on the baking paper. If serving warm, cut into portions straight away, otherwise allow to cool completely and cut into portions when cold. To reheat the fudge sauce, transfer to a saucepan and gently heat through, or pierce the cling film and heat in the microwave. Arrange the warm or cold brownies on plates, pour the hot fudge sauce over the top and serve with scoops of ice cream or whipped cream.

Coconut & Lime Meringue Pie

Serves 6–8

As this pastry is so short and crumbly, it may break up when you are trying to roll it out. If this happens, try coarsely grating it directly into the tin and then quickly press it up the sides and into the shape of the tin. No one will know the difference!

To make the pastry, place the butter, flour, salt and sugar into a food processor and blend for 20 seconds. Alternatively, you can rub together by hand. Add the egg yolk and cream and blend again or mix until the dough just comes together. Do not overwork the dough or the pastry will be tough. Wrap the pastry in cling film and chill for 1 hour.

Grease a 20cm (8in) round, fluted, loose-bottomed flan tin, of 3cm (1¼in) in depth. Roll out the pastry on a lightly floured work surface and use it to line the prepared tin. Trim the edges and prick the base with a fork, then chill for about 20 minutes.

Preheat the oven to 200°C (400°F), gas mark 6. Line the pastry case with foil or non-stick baking paper and a thin layer of baking beans. Bake 'blind' for 15–20 minutes, then take the pastry case out of the oven and reduce the temperature to 180°C (350°F), gas mark 4.

Carefully remove the beans and the foil or paper from the case, then return it to the oven for 3–5 minutes until lightly golden.

While the pastry is blind baking, make the filling. Place the lime zest and juice in a saucepan with the vanilla seeds, sugar and coconut milk, then heat gently until the sugar dissolves.

Mix the cornflour in a small bowl with 4 tablespoons of cold water, then stir it into the coconut mixture. Bring to the boil and cook for 2–3 minutes until thickened, stirring constantly. Remove from the heat and then allow to cool slightly. »

For the pastry

100g (4oz) butter, chilled and diced, plus extra for greasing

175g (6oz) plain flour, plus extra for dusting

pinch of salt

50g (2oz) caster sugar

1 egg yolk

½ tbsp double cream

For the filling

finely grated zest and juice of 3 limes

seeds scraped from 1 vanilla pod

175g (6oz) caster sugar

400g tin of coconut milk

4 tbsp cornflour

4 egg yolks

50g (2oz) butter, softened

For the meringue

2 egg whites

100g (4oz) caster sugar

whipped cream, to serve

Finally, beat in the egg yolks and butter and return to the heat to cook gently for 6–8 minutes, stirring constantly, until thick enough to coat the back of a spoon. Pour the filling into the pastry case and allow to cool completely.

Once the filling is cool, preheat the oven to 180°C (350°F), gas mark 4. To make the meringue, place the egg whites in a large bowl and whisk into soft peaks, then gradually whisk in the sugar a spoonful at a time to make a stiff, glossy meringue. Spoon the meringue on top of the filling, spreading it out evenly to make sure it forms a good seal with the pastry edge. Swirl the top of the meringue with the tip of a knife and bake the pie for 15 minutes or until it is lightly golden and crisp on top.

Allow the pie to cool slightly and then carefully remove the tart from the tin. Allow to cool completely before chilling for a few hours or overnight until completely set. To serve, cut into slices and arrange on plates with whipped cream.

Mini Bakewell Tarts

Be careful not to overfill the pastry cases for these mini tarts as the filling will rise while it is cooking. You can vary the jam filling depending on what's available – apricot or peach are both delicious, as is rhubarb and ginger. These tarts are shown in the picture on page 197.

50g (2oz) butter, plus extra for greasing

250g (9oz) Sweet Shortcrust Pastry (see page 216)

plain flour, for dusting

125g (4½oz) raspberry or strawberry jam

50g (2oz) icing sugar, plus extra for dusting

1 egg

125g (4½oz) ground almonds

few drops of vanilla extract

50g (2oz) flaked almonds

Preheat the oven to 200°C (400°F), gas mark 6. Grease two 12-hole mini muffin tins.

Roll out the pastry on a lightly floured work surface and stamp out circles with a 5cm (2in) straight-sided cutter. Use to line the moulds, carefully pressing down and removing any air bubbles; the pastry should only come halfway up the sides. Spoon ½ teaspoon of jam into the bottom of each lined pastry case. Chill for at least 30 minutes to allow the pastry to rest.

Meanwhile, use an electric beater to beat the butter and icing sugar together in a medium-sized bowl for 1–2 minutes until pale and fluffy. Beat in the egg, ground almonds and vanilla extract to make a paste. This will keep for 2 weeks in the fridge.

Spoon the almond paste on top of the jam, filling the tarts almost to the top, and spread evenly with a small knife or palette knife. Scatter over the flaked almonds and bake for 12–15 minutes until puffed up and lightly golden.

Leave in the muffin tins for a few minutes to cool. Then carefully transfer the tarts to a wire rack to cool completely, releasing them with the help of a small knife, but being careful that the top doesn't separate from the bottom.

Dust with icing sugar and arrange on plates to serve.

Orange & Vanilla Madeleines

For these dainty, shell-shaped cakes you'll need a Madeleine tin with 4 x 4.5cm (1½ x 1¾in) holes, available from specialist cookware shops or by mail order. The cakes are best eaten on the day they are cooked but the raw mixture will keep in the fridge for a couple of weeks, so make them as you need them.

50g (2oz) butter, diced, plus extra for greasing
25g (1oz) plain flour, plus extra for dusting
seeds scraped from ¼ vanilla pod
1 egg white, at room temperature
½ tsp finely grated orange zest
50g (2oz) icing sugar, sifted
25g (1oz) ground almonds
50g (2oz) toasted skinned hazelnuts, roughly chopped

Lightly grease a 24-hole Madeleine tin with softened butter, then dust with flour, shaking off any excess. Place in the fridge for at least 2 hours to set.

Place the butter in a small saucepan, allow it to melt and then simmer for about 6–8 minutes until it is really dark brown, stirring occasionally and being careful of spitting (it will be the colour of a toasted nut, with lots of bits in it, but should not smell burnt). Remove from the heat and allow to cool.

Sift the flour into a large bowl. Add the vanilla seeds, egg white, orange zest, sifted icing sugar and ground almonds. Using an electric beater, beat the ingredients until well combined and smooth. Gradually add the brown, melted butter and slowly mix for 4–5 minutes until the mixture is smooth and thickened. Spoon the mixture into a piping bag fitted with a 2cm (¾in) plain nozzle and chill the bag in the fridge for at least 2 hours until firm.

When ready to cook, preheat the oven to 180°C (350°F), gas mark 4. Pipe the mixture into the moulds, releasing it from the nozzle with a knife dipped in warm water and using the knife to spread the mixture a little in the tin. Don't worry if the mixture doesn't completely fill the moulds as it will spread when cooking. Sprinkle the hazelnuts on top.

Bake for 10–12 minutes until well risen, golden and springy to the touch. Remove from the oven and allow to rest in the tin for 2 minutes, then ease out of the tins with the tip of a knife and leave on a wire rack to cool slightly.

To serve, arrange on plates and enjoy with coffee or a cup of tea.

MacNean Mint Chocolate Truffles

Makes 30

Shown on page 197, these truffles make wonderful gifts for friends (if you can bear to give them away...!). For a different flavour, add rum, Cointreau or whiskey instead of the crème de menthe and mint.

100ml (4fl oz) double cream
1 tbsp crème de menthe
1 tbsp chopped mint
225g (8oz) plain chocolate (minimum 55% cocoa solids), broken into squares
125g (4½oz) butter, diced

For the coating

50g (2oz) plain chocolate (minimum 55% cocoa solids), broken into squares
25g (1oz) good-quality cocoa powder

Place the cream in a small saucepan with the crème de menthe and mint. Bring to the boil, then remove from the heat and allow to cool. Set aside for 1 hour to allow the flavours to infuse.

Pour the infused cream through a sieve into a small, clean saucepan and bring to the boil. Reduce the heat, then whisk in the chocolate and butter until smooth and melted. Place in a bowl, cover with cling film and then allow to cool in the fridge for 2–3 hours until the mixture is cold and set.

Remove the set mixture from the fridge about 30 minutes before you intend to use it. Scoop the mixture into thirty even-sized balls – a large melon baller is best for this, or use a teaspoon. Make sure to dip the melon baller in hot water between each scoop to make the job easier. Arrange the truffles on a baking sheet lined with non-stick baking paper. Wearing clean rubber gloves, and with cold hands, shape the balls until slightly more rounded. Chill the baking sheet of balls in the fridge.

To make the coating, melt the chocolate in a heatproof bowl set over a saucepan of simmering water or in the microwave. Set aside to cool a little. Sift the cocoa powder into a small bowl.

Again, wearing clean rubber gloves, dip the tips of your fingers in the melted chocolate and rub all over a truffle to lightly coat. Toss in the cocoa powder until completely coated and then arrange on a clean baking sheet lined with non-stick baking paper. Repeat until all the truffles are coated. Cover with cling film and chill until needed. These will keep happily in the fridge for up to 2 weeks.

To serve, arrange the truffles on a plate or platter.

Coconut Tuilles

Makes about 40

25g (1oz) butter

25g (1oz) icing sugar

25g (1oz) plain flour

2 tbsp desiccated coconut

1 egg white

1 tsp runny honey

¼ tsp vanilla extract

These are shown in the picture on page 197. They can be stored for up to 3 days in an airtight container. Alternatively, you can freeze the uncooked mixture in plastic bags for up to 1 month, so that you can make a few at a time whenever you fancy them. Allow the mixture to thaw for an hour before cooking.

Melt the butter in a small saucepan or in the microwave. Set aside to cool a little.

Sift the icing sugar and flour into a bowl and stir in the desiccated coconut. Make a well in the centre and add the egg white, honey and vanilla extract. Mix well to combine, gradually pour in the melted butter and mix again until smooth. Cover with cling film and place in the fridge for at least 2 hours.

Preheat the oven to 180°C (350°F), gas mark 4. Line a couple of baking sheets with non-stick baking paper and use a pencil to mark out 5cm (2in) circles.

Carefully spread a teaspoonful of mixture into each circle with a small palette knife or the back of teaspoon which has been dipped in hot water. Bake for about 5 minutes or until golden brown.

Remove from the oven and quickly transfer to a tuille tray, if available, or place each biscuit over a rolling pin to shape – the circles should be curled down on either side to look like one half of a tube. Arrange the tuilles on a plate to serve.

Jammy Dodgers

Makes 16–18

These are shown in the picture on page 197. They are best eaten on the same day they are made. If you do wish to make them in advance, keep the shortcake in an airtight container and fill with the jam just before serving.

To make the shortcake, sift the flour and icing sugar into a bowl. Stir in the lime zest, then beat in the butter with a wooden spoon to give rough crumbs. Bring the mixture together with your hands to form a soft, smooth dough. Wrap in cling film and chill for at least 30 minutes, or for up to 3 days is fine.

To make the jam filling, place the jam, vanilla extract and crème de cassis in a small saucepan and simmer over a low heat for 8–10 minutes until melted and slightly thickened. Allow to cool completely. This can be stored in your fridge covered with cling film for up to 1 month.

Preheat the oven to 190°C (375°F), gas mark 5. Roll out the dough on a lightly floured work surface to a thickness of 3mm (⅛in). Stamp out about 32–36 circles using a 4cm (1½in) fluted cutter and arrange on baking sheets lined with non-stick baking paper.

Then, using a 1cm (½in) plain nozzle (a metal rather than plastic one is best for this) stamp out holes in the centre of half of the circles (this will allow the jam to show through later). Bake the biscuits for about 8–10 minutes until crisp and lightly golden.

To assemble, spoon a teaspoon of the jam mixture on to the centre of each unstamped shortcake. Dust the remaining shortcakes with icing sugar and then place on the jam-topped biscuits, pressing down lightly so that the jam squeezes out just a little bit through the hole. Arrange on plates to serve.

For the shortcake

75g (3oz) plain flour, plus extra for dusting

25g (1oz) icing sugar, plus extra for dusting

finely grated zest of 1 lime

50g (2oz) butter, softened

For the filling

100g (4oz) raspberry or strawberry jam

¼ tsp vanilla extract (preferably good-quality with seeds)

1 tbsp crème de cassis (blackcurrant liqueur)

Drinks

Cosmopolitan

Serves 4

150ml (¼ pint) vodka
110ml (4fl oz) Cointreau
50ml (2fl oz) fresh lime juice
50ml (2fl oz) cranberry juice
ice, to serve
strip of orange peel, cut with a vegetable swivel peeler, to decorate

The classic Cosmopolitan is best known for its role in the TV show, Sex and the City! There are hundreds of variations on the Cosmo, using different amounts of cranberry juice, some with Triple Sec instead of Cointreau, and others with a citrus vodka. It's all a matter of personal preference; this is the way I like it.

Fill a cocktail shaker two-thirds full with ice and then pour in the vodka, Cointreau, lime juice and cranberry juice. Shake until well combined and then strain into chilled martini-style glasses. Decorate with a strip of orange peel to serve.

Apple & Mint Vodka

Serves 4

small bunch of mint
2 Granny Smiths apples, cored and sliced
1 tbsp caster sugar
200ml (7fl oz) vodka
450ml (16fl oz) tonic water or soda water
plenty of ice, to serve

Don't get too carried away, as this wonderfully refreshing drink goes down very easily! You can use any variety of apples but I prefer the slight sharpness of Granny Smiths. You may need to alter the amount of sugar depending on how sweet the apples are.

Set aside four sprigs of the mint to decorate the glasses and place the remaining leaves along with the apple slices and sugar in either a cocktail shaker or a sturdy jug.

Use the end of a rolling pin to smash the apple and mint together into a lumpy pulp. Pour in the vodka and a handful of ice and shake until well combined. If using a jug, simply stir well with a spoon.

Half-fill four tall glasses with ice and strain the flavoured vodka over, top up with tonic or soda water and decorate with the reserved mint sprigs.

Classic Pimm's Cocktail

Serves 8

This must be one of the best cocktails for a hot summer's day. It was traditionally served on the lawn at English garden parties, but these days it's essential for barbecues or picnics. For a more tropical twist, replace the lemonade with ginger beer.

2 crisp eating apples, cored and thinly sliced
½ cucumber, cut into thin slices
6 large mint sprigs, leaves stripped
70cl bottle Pimm's No.1
1 litre (1¾ pints) lemonade
plenty of ice, to serve

Place a couple of apple and cucumber slices in eight tall glasses, add a few mint leaves, then fill each glass two-thirds full of ice. Mix the Pimm's in a large jug with enough lemonade to taste, a couple of handfuls of ice and the rest of the apple, cucumber and mint leaves. Stir well to combine and pour into the glasses to serve.

Spicy Bloody Mary

Serves 6–8

Make this with tomato juice from a tin, as it's much thinner than juice from a carton. The secret is in the balance of the seasoning, which you'll just have to experiment with to find the perfect balance for you. If you want to serve it the traditional way, garnish the glasses with a celery stick. Remember that the Worcestershire sauce means that this drink is not suitable for vegetarians.

800g tin of tomato juice (or use a carton of thin tomato juice)
1–2 tbsp Worcestershire sauce
½–1 tsp Tabasco sauce
1–1½ tsp celery salt
juice of 1–2 limes
2 tsp grated horseradish (optional)
150ml (¼ pint) vodka
50ml (2fl oz) dry fino sherry
plenty of crushed ice and celery sticks (optional), to serve

Place the tomato juice in a large cocktail shaker with 1 tablespoon of Worcestershire sauce, ½ teaspoon of Tabasco sauce, 1 teaspoon of celery salt, the juice of a lime and grated horseradish, if using. Fill the shaker with ice and shake until well chilled. Add the vodka and sherry, then shake again to thoroughly combine. Taste and adjust the seasoning, adding more Worcestershire sauce, Tabasco sauce, celery salt and lime juice as required. Strain into tall, sturdy glasses, top with crushed ice and add swizzle sticks or celery sticks to serve.

Sangria

Serves 6

---

2 small oranges, sliced

1 small lemon, sliced

juice of 2 lemons

40g (1½oz) caster sugar

300ml (11fl oz) fruity red wine, (e.g. Beaujolais)

120ml (4½fl oz) brandy

300ml (11fl oz) sparkling mineral water or lemonade

plenty of ice, to serve

This classic Spanish drink always conjures up memories of relaxing holidays and hot sunshine. For a Mexican twist, replace the brandy with Tequila and use lime juice instead of lemon juice.

Place the orange and lemon slices in a large jug and then fill it two-thirds of the way up with ice. Put the lemon juice in a small pan, mix in the sugar, heat and simmer gently for 1–2 minutes until it has dissolved. Remove from the heat and add the wine, then pour the liquid into the jug and stir in the brandy and sparkling water or lemonade. Serve in tall glasses.

Peach Bellini

Serves 4

---

2 large ripe peaches or 4 tinned peach halves

1 tbsp caster sugar

2 tbsp brandy

½ bottle Champagne or sparkling wine, chilled

This drink originates from Harry's Bar in Venice, where the peaches are finely chopped by hand in front of you. The barmen would be horrified, but I find that a tin of drained peaches works just as well when fresh are unavailable. If it's a special occasion, sugar the rims of the glasses by wiping a small piece of peach around the rims to make them sticky, then dip in caster sugar!

Peel and stone the fresh peaches and cut them into slices. Blend the fresh peach flesh or tinned peach halves with the sugar and brandy until smooth. If you have a mini hand-held blender, this is ideal; if not, use a fork to mash the flesh as smoothly as possible.

Divide the purée between four Champagne flutes or glasses, top up with the chilled Champagne or sparkling wine and serve immediately.

The Best Ever Irish Coffee

Serves 2

I've perfected this recipe over time and believe it really is the best ever Irish coffee. Heat the glasses if you can be bothered (to keep the coffee hot for longer), by pouring boiling water over them from a kettle, and turning them carefully so that they do not crack. Or you could take glasses straight from the dishwasher while still piping hot.

75ml (3fl oz) double cream, well chilled
2 tbsp light muscovado sugar
2 tbsp whiskey
2 tbsp Baileys
2 tbsp Kahlúa (coffee liqueur)
300ml (11fl oz) freshly brewed piping hot espresso coffee
pinch of freshly grated nutmeg, to decorate

Place the cream in a bowl and whip lightly, then chill until needed.

Heat a small, heavy-based frying pan over a medium heat. Sprinkle the sugar over the base of the frying pan and heat for 1 minute, without stirring – the sugar will caramelise. Pour in the whiskey and quickly light with a match or flambé – the sugar will seize and harden, but don't worry as it will melt again once the flames die down. Stir in the Baileys and Kahlúa and cook over a high heat for 3–4 minutes until smooth, stirring constantly to help the sugar dissolve.

Divide the alcohol mixture between two hefty, thick-stemmed glasses, (both about 250ml/9fl oz in capacity) and then carefully pour in the coffee. Then, over the back of a metal spoon, carefully pour a layer of cream on top (the spoon trick really is worth doing as it helps prevent the cream from sinking). Add a tiny grating of nutmeg and serve at once.

Larder

A Well-stocked Larder

This book wouldn't be complete without a good larder chapter. Stocks and sauces are so important – I think of them as the body and soul of my cooking. In this section you'll find some of the most basic sauces and condiments that are worth making and keeping in the fridge for when needed. I've also included some of the delicious sauces that we serve at MacNean, as well as the four basic stocks that are used in recipes throughout this book.

Many of my recipes use shortcrust pastry, and homemade is much better, so this section has instructions for making your own. Puff pastry, however, can be tricky to make, and store-bought all-butter versions are excellent, so I recommend you buy this. And although vegetable accompaniments are included with most of my recipes, I've put two of the most essential ones in this chapter; root vegetables and potatoes are both invaluable to keep in your larder, ready to turn into a delicious side dish at any time.

To sterilise jars or bottles, wash well in really hot soapy water, rinse thoroughly, then dry in a warm oven. Alternatively, you could put them through a dishwasher cycle. When sterilised, fill with the contents immediately, and seal tightly.

Pesto

This will keep happily in the fridge for up to 1 week – just keep it topped up with a little extra olive oil to ensure it stays tasting lovely and fresh. It's great stirred into pasta for an instant simple supper.

Place the basil in a food processor with the garlic, pine nuts and a quarter of the olive oil. Blend to a paste, then slowly add the remaining olive oil through the feeder tube.

Transfer to a bowl and fold in the Parmesan, then season with salt and pepper to taste. Cover with cling film and chill until needed.

Varation

Sun-dried Tomato Pesto

Reduce the quantity of basil to 8 leaves and add 175g (6oz) semi sun-dried or sun blush tomatoes. Omit the Parmesan and blend for 2 minutes, then season with salt and pepper to taste. Makes 300ml (11fl oz).

Makes 250ml (9fl oz)
Vegetarian

1 large bunch of basil leaves (at least 50g/2oz)
2 garlic cloves, peeled and chopped
25g (1oz) pine nuts, toasted
175ml (6fl oz) extra virgin olive oil
50g (2oz) freshly grated Parmesan cheese
Maldon sea salt and freshly ground black pepper

Red Onion Marmalade

This can be used in so many ways and will keep for up to 2 weeks in the fridge. We get through a lot of it in the restaurant and at home I love it with cold meats or in a simple cheese sandwich.

Makes 450ml (1lb)
Vegetarian

2 tbsp olive oil
5 red onions, peeled and thinly sliced
1 garlic clove, peeled and crushed
2 tsp light muscovado sugar
200ml (7fl oz) red wine
2 tbsp balsamic vinegar
salt and freshly ground black pepper

Heat the olive oil in a large saucepan over a low heat, add the onions and cook for about 10 minutes, stirring occasionally, until soft but not browned.

Stir in the garlic and sugar and then pour in the red wine and balsamic vinegar. Cook gently for about 35–40 minutes until thickened and sticky, stirring occasionally. Season with salt and pepper to taste.

Store the marmalade in an airtight container or sterilised jar (see opposite page) in the fridge and use as required.

Mayonnaise

This takes just minutes to make and will keep in the fridge for up to 1 week. A number of different flavourings are also listed below.

Makes 250ml (9fl oz)
Vegetarian

1 egg, at room temperature
2 tsp white wine vinegar
pinch of caster sugar
1 tsp Dijon mustard
100ml (4fl oz) olive oil
100ml (4fl oz) sunflower oil
salt and freshly ground white pepper

Break the egg into the food processor and add ½ teaspoon of salt, the vinegar, sugar, mustard and half of the olive oil. Whiz for 10 seconds.

Leave the mixture to stand for a couple of seconds, then turn the processor on again and pour the remaining olive oil and the sunflower oil through the feeder tube in a thin, steady stream. This should take 25–30 seconds.

Switch off the machine, take off the lid, scrape down the sides, and whiz again for 2–3 seconds. Transfer to a bowl or a jar, season with salt and pepper to taste and cover with cling film. Chill until ready to use.

Variations

Aïoli

Add two chopped garlic cloves to the food processor with the egg.

Garlic & Chive Mayonnaise

Stir two crushed garlic cloves and 2 tablespoons of snipped fresh chives into 150ml (¼ pint) of the mayonnaise.

Lemon Mayonnaise

Combine 250ml (9fl oz) of mayonnaise with the juice and rind of one small lemon and 1 tablespoon of snipped fresh chives.

Béchamel Sauce

This classic white sauce is easy to make, so I've never understood why they sell dehydrated packets of it in the supermarket! Depending on what you intend to put it with, the sauce can be flavoured with chopped flat-leaf parsley or snipped chives, a dollop of your favourite mustard or a handful of grated cheese. You can also replace some of the milk with stock for a lighter result.

Makes about 300ml (11fl oz)
Vegetarian

450ml (16fl oz) milk
1 small onion, peeled and roughly chopped
1 fresh bay leaf
½ tsp black peppercorns
25g (1oz) butter
25g (1oz) plain flour
pinch of freshly grated nutmeg
salt and freshly ground white pepper

Place the milk in a small saucepan with the onion, bay leaf and peppercorns. Bring to scalding point, then remove from the heat, cover and allow to infuse for at least 10, or for up to 30 minutes. Strain through a sieve into a jug.

Wipe out the saucepan with kitchen paper and melt the butter over a medium heat. Stir in the flour and cook for 1 minute, stirring constantly with a wooden spoon. Remove the saucepan from the heat and gradually pour in the infused milk, whisking until smooth after each addition. Season with salt and pepper to taste and add a pinch of nutmeg.

Return the pan to the heat and bring the sauce to the boil, whisking constantly. Then reduce the heat and simmer gently for 5 minutes, stirring occasionally, until the sauce is smooth and thickened enough to coat the back of a wooden spoon,

Use immediately or transfer to a jug, cover with cling film, pressing it into the top of the sauce to prevent a skin forming, and allow to cool. Keep in the fridge for up to 2 days and reheat slowly in a saucepan over a low heat.

Red Wine Sauce

This is especially delicious with pork dishes, such as Marinated Pork Fillet with Basil & Pine Nut Stuffing (see page 148). I always make it in large batches and freeze in small containers so it's there when I need it.

Makes about 75ml (3fl oz)

1 tbsp balsamic vinegar
150ml (¼ pint) red wine
1 heaped tsp light muscovado sugar
150ml (¼ pint) beef stock (see page 218)
1 tsp chopped thyme
salt and freshly ground black pepper

Heat a small saucepan and pour in the vinegar and red wine. Boil for about 5 minutes or until reduced by half. Add the sugar, stock and thyme and reduce again for another 10–12 minutes or so or until you have achieved a good sauce consistency, stirring occasionally. Leave to cool, then season with salt and pepper to taste, strain into a bowl, cover with cling film and use as required. This will keep for 1 week in the fridge.

Madeira Sauce

This has to be one of the nicest sauces that we use in the restaurant. It's a vital element of my signature lamb recipe, Loin of Lamb in Crisp Potato Crust (see page 144). It keeps for up to 3 days in the fridge if stored in a rigid plastic container, and it also freezes well.

Pour the balsamic vinegar into a small saucepan and stir in the sugar. Bring to the boil, then reduce to a simmer, and cook over a medium heat for about 2 minutes or until the vinegar and sugar are reduced to a syrup. Add the Madeira and red wine and return to a simmer for about 6–8 minutes until the sauce has reduced by half.

Add the beef stock and thyme to the sauce and reduce it again for about 20 minutes until the sauce is thick and glossy and has become more concentrated in flavour.

Season the sauce with salt and pepper to taste. Use immediately or cool and store in the fridge or freezer in a lidded plastic container.

Makes 200ml (7fl oz)

1 tbsp balsamic vinegar
1 tbsp light muscovado sugar
200ml (7fl oz) Madeira
100ml (3½fl oz) red wine
600ml (1 pint) beef stock (see page 218)
1 tsp chopped thyme leaves
salt and freshly ground black pepper

Blue Cheese & Celery Sauce

This goes extremely well with a well-cooked beef steak or pan-fried pork steaks. It can be made well in advance and gently reheated just before serving.

Heat a small saucepan over a medium heat and add the olive oil and butter. Once the butter has melted and is foaming, add the onion and celery. Cook for 2–3 minutes until the onion has softened and the celery is tender, stirring occasionally.

Pour the port and wine into the celery mixture, then use a match to ignite the port. It will flare up for about 5–10 seconds and then subside when the alcohol flame burns off. When the alcohol has burnt off, stir in the stock and slowly add the cream. Simmer for about 10 minutes until reduced, thickened and darkened in colour. Stir in the cheese until melted, then season with salt and pepper to taste.

Serve at once or allow the sauce to cool down completely and store in a bowl in the fridge, covered with cling film, for up to 2 days. Reheat gently in a saucepan over a low heat when needed.

Makes about 250ml (9fl oz)

1 tbsp olive oil
large knob of butter
1 small onion, peeled and finely chopped
2 small celery sticks, thinly sliced
100ml (3½fl oz) ruby red port
100ml (3½fl oz) dry white wine
100ml (3½fl oz) beef stock (see page 218)
100ml (3½fl oz) double cream
100g (4oz) blue cheese, rind removed and crumbled (e.g. Cashel blue)
salt and freshly ground black pepper

Sauce Diane

My mother taught me to make this classic sauce and I like to serve it with steak. It is also good with pan-fried pork or lamb chops, or over a chicken breast. It is fairly rich so you really don't need much of it – a little goes a long way.

Heat a medium-sized saucepan over a medium heat and add 1 tablespoon of the olive oil and all of the butter, then swirl the pan until the butter has melted and is foaming. Tip in the shallot and mushrooms and sauté for 2–3 minutes until tender.

Pour over the brandy, then use a match to ignite the alcohol. It will flare up for about 5–10 seconds and then subside when the flame burns off. Add the wine and simmer until reduced by half.

Stir the stock into the saucepan with the Worcestershire sauce, sugar and cream. Bring to the boil, then turn down the heat and simmer for 20–25 minutes, stirring occasionally, until thickened and reduced to a consistency which will coat the back of a wooden spoon.

Stir in the parsley and lemon juice. Season the sauce with salt and pepper to taste. Use immediately or allow the sauce to cool down completely and store in a bowl in the fridge, covered with cling film, for up to 2 days. Reheat gently in a saucepan over a low heat when needed.

Makes about 275ml (10fl oz)

2 tbsp olive oil

25g (1oz) butter

1 shallot, peeled and finely chopped

150g (5oz) button mushrooms, brushed/wiped and sliced

100ml (4fl oz) brandy

150ml (¼ pint) white wine

150ml (¼ pint) beef stock (see page 218)

1 tbsp Worcestershire sauce

good pinch of caster sugar

150ml (¼ pint) double cream

1 tbsp chopped flat-leaf parsley

squeeze of fresh lemon juice

salt and freshly ground black pepper

Honey & Clove Sauce

This sauce keeps for up to a week in a rigid plastic container in the fridge. If you want to serve it with the Duck Confit (see page 122), then make double the quantity. It is also good with roast pork or chicken.

Place all the ingredients, apart from the seasoning, in a small saucepan. Bring to the boil, then reduce the heat and simmer vigorously for 5 minutes or until the mixture has thickened to a sauce consistency which will coat the back of a wooden spoon.

Season with salt and pepper to taste, then pass the sauce through a sieve into a clean saucepan. Reheat gently and use immediately, or cool and store in the fridge in a lidded plastic container.

Makes about 200ml (7fl oz)

4 tbsp runny honey

2 tbsp dark soy sauce

2 tbsp balsamic vinegar

2 tbsp light muscovado sugar

2 tbsp tomato ketchup

2 tsp whole cloves

225ml (8fl oz) beef stock (see page 218)

salt and freshly ground black pepper

Wild Mushroom Sauce

This very versatile sauce is used regularly in the restaurant, especially in the autumn when wild mushrooms are at their best. It goes well with fish, lamb, pork and steak – almost anything really! Of course, the taste of the sauce will only be as good as the selection of wild mushrooms you use, so it is worth looking out for the stronger flavoured varieties, such as ceps or chanterelle.

Heat a medium-sized saucepan over a medium heat and add the butter. When it is foaming, add the shallots, garlic, mushrooms and thyme. Cook for 4–5 minutes until softened but not browned and then pour in the Madeira and allow it to bubble and reduce right down. This should take about 5 minutes.

When there is no liquid left, stir in the stock and double cream. Bring to the boil, then turn down the heat and simmer for 8 minutes until reduced a little. Purée the sauce with a hand-held blender and season with salt and pepper to taste.

Serve at once or allow the sauce to cool down completely and store in a bowl in the fridge, covered with cling film, for up to 2 days. Reheat gently in a saucepan over a low heat when needed.

Makes about 450ml (16 fl oz)

25g (1oz) butter
2 shallots, peeled and diced
1 garlic clove, peeled and crushed
100g (4oz) wild mushrooms, trimmed and diced (e.g. ceps, chanterelle, shiitake and oyster)
1 tsp chopped thyme leaves
100ml (3½fl oz) Madeira
225ml (8fl oz) chicken stock (see page 219)
175ml (6fl oz) double cream
salt and freshly ground black pepper

Balsamic Cream

I tend to serve this with seared scallops, roasted duck or as part of my Spicy Chicken Salad (see page 79), but it also works well with pan-fried pork or lamb chops, or even steak. Vary the type of stock you use depending on what you are serving it with.

Place the stock in a small saucepan with the tomato purée, vinegar and cream. Bring to the boil, then reduce the heat and simmer for 10–15 minutes until reduced by a quarter and thickened to a sauce consistency.

Season with salt and pepper to taste. Use immediately or allow to cool, transfer to a bowl and cover with cling film, then chill until needed, for up to 5 days.

Makes 150ml (¼ pint)

150ml (¼ pint) beef or chicken stock (see pages 218 and 219)
1 tbsp tomato purée
2 tbsp balsamic vinegar
150ml (¼ pint) double cream
salt and freshly ground black pepper

Port & Balsamic Syrup

We use this sauce daily in the restaurant. I always serve it cold, with grilled fish, goat's cheese, pan-fried foie gras or chicken liver pâté. This will keep for 2–3 months in the fridge. When you want to use it, if you find it has solidified too much, add a few drops of boiling water, stirring to loosen.

Place the port in a small, heavy-based saucepan with the balsamic vinegar, Madeira and sugar. Bring to the boil, then turn down the heat and simmer for 20 minutes until reduced by a third and when the mixture has become thick and syrupy, like runny honey.

Allow to cool down completely before serving, then store in a bowl in the fridge, covered with cling film, for up to 2 days.

Makes 120ml (4½fl oz)
Vegetarian

100ml (3½fl oz) ruby red port

100ml (3½fl oz) balsamic vinegar

100ml (3½fl oz) Madeira

100g (4oz) caster sugar

Tomato Sauce

This staple recipe can be used for making pizzas, pasta toppings and so much more. You can also use it to make my Twister Bread Rolls (see page 46). If tomatoes are not in season, it is much better to use a can of chopped tomatoes rather than bland, out-of-season ones – otherwise you could end with very tasteless mush! The sauce will keep happily in the fridge for up to 1 week covered with cling film.

Heat the olive oil in a medium-sized saucepan over a medium heat and sauté the onion and garlic for a few minutes until softened but not browned. Tip in the tomatoes, vinegar, sugar and tomato purée. Cook over a low heat for a few minutes, stirring constantly to help break the tomatoes down. Season with salt and pepper to taste. Simmer gently for about 25–30 minutes until the sauce has reduced and dried out a little.

Use immediately or allow to cool, transfer to a bowl and cover with cling film, then chill until needed.

Makes 350ml (12fl oz)
Vegetarian

1 tbsp olive oil

1 onion, peeled and finely chopped

1 garlic clove, peeled and crushed

6 large ripe tomatoes, peeled, deseeded and cut into chunks, or 400g tin of chopped tomatoes

2 tsp red wine vinegar

1 tsp caster sugar

2 tsp tomato purée

Maldon sea salt and freshly ground black pepper

Tapenade

This delicious olive paste is great simply spread on bruschetta. I also like to serve it on crostini with a rack of lamb and some wilted spinach. It is excellent smeared under the skin of a chicken breast before roasting or as part of a Mediterranean sandwich.

Place the olives in a food processor along with the lemon juice, capers, anchovy fillets, garlic and parsley. Pulse until just combined, then pour in enough of the olive oil to make a smooth purée. Season with salt and pepper to taste.

This will keep in the fridge, in a sterilised jar (see page 208), for up to 1 week.

Makes about 400g (14oz)

250g (9oz) good-quality pitted black olives

juice of 1 lemon

3 tbsp capers, drained and rinsed

6 anchovy fillets, drained

1 garlic clove, peeled

2 tbsp roughly chopped flat-leaf parsley

90–100ml (3½–4fl oz) extra virgin olive oil

salt and freshly ground black pepper

Chilli Jam

One of my store-cupboard essentials, this is simple to make and nicer than shop-bought sweet chilli sauce. It lasts in the fridge for up to 3 weeks and can be kept in a squeezy plastic bottle for garnishing plates. It's delicious served with seafood, such as Prawns in Kataifi Pastry (see page 70).

Heat the olive oil in a heavy-based saucepan over a medium heat. Add the onions, red peppers and garlic and sauté for 2 minutes until they are just beginning to soften. Stir in the chilli and tomato purée and cook for 3 minutes, stirring occasionally.

Stir in the balsamic vinegar, sugar, tomatoes and soy sauce and pour in 300ml (11fl oz) of water to just cover. Simmer for 45–50 minutes until well reduced and thickened, stirring occasionally.

Remove the chilli jam from the heat and allow to cool completely, then tip into a food processor or blender and blend to a purée. Pass through a sieve set over a bowl and season with salt and pepper to taste. Transfer to a rigid plastic container or squeezy plastic bottle and store in the fridge.

Makes about 450ml (16fl oz)
Vegetarian

2 tbsp olive oil

2 onions, peeled and roughly diced

2 red peppers, deseeded and roughly diced

1 garlic clove, peeled and crushed

1 red chilli, deseeded and finely chopped

1 tbsp tomato purée

1 tbsp balsamic vinegar

50g (2oz) light muscovado sugar

4 ripe tomatoes, diced

1 tbsp dark soy sauce

Maldon sea salt and freshly ground black pepper

Shortcrust Pastry

This pastry takes very little time to make and is infinitely better than any shop-bought varieties. It freezes very well so can be made in batches to keep frozen until needed.

Sift the flour and salt into a food processor, add the chilled butter and the lard or white vegetable fat and process for a few seconds until the mixture looks like fine breadcrumbs. Tip into a bowl, add 1½ tbsp cold water, and stir with a round-bladed knife until the mixture just starts to stick together. Gather the dough into a ball with your hands and knead briefly on a lightly floured work surface until smooth. Chill in the fridge for at least 30 minutes before using.

If you don't wish to use immediately, wrap in cling film and store in the fridge for up to 2 days, or wrap in freezer film and freeze it.

Makes 375g (13oz)

225g (8oz) plain flour, plus extra for dusting

½ tsp salt

60g (2½oz) unsalted butter, cut into small pieces and chilled

60g (2½oz) lard or white vegetable fat, cut into small pieces and chilled

Sweet Shortcrust Pastry

Use this sweeter version of shortcrust pastry for making desserts.

Put the flour, butter and icing sugar into a food processor and blend together until the mixture looks like breadcrumbs. Add the egg and whiz briefly until the mixture just starts to stick together into a ball. Wrap the ball in cling film and chill in the fridge for at least 10 minutes or for up to 30 minutes before rolling it.

Turn the dough on to a lightly floured work surface and knead very briefly until smooth. Roll out as required, then chill again in the fridge for at least 20 minutes before baking. If not using the pastry immediately, it will keep for up to 2 days in the fridge, or wrap it in freezer film and store in the freezer.

Makes 475g (1lb 1oz)
Vegetarian

225g (8oz) plain flour, plus extra for dusting

100g (4oz) chilled unsalted butter, cut into small pieces

100g (4oz) icing sugar, sifted

1 egg

Roasted Root Vegetables

Don't overcrowd the vegetables in the roasting tin or they will stew rather than roast. If necessary, use two smaller tins and put on separate oven shelves, swapping over halfway through the cooking time. These are great served with Coq au Vin (see page 124).

Preheat the oven to 180°C (350°F), gas mark 4. Place the olive oil in a large roasting tin, add the carrots and parsnips and toss until well coated in the oil. Season the vegetables generously with salt and pepper. Roast for 40 minutes until they are almost tender, stirring occasionally.

Remove the root vegetables from the oven and increase the oven temperature to 200°C (400°F), gas mark 6. Add the honey, soy sauce and chilli to the tin, tossing to coat evenly.

Once the oven has reached the higher temperature, return the tin to the oven and roast for another 10–15 minutes or until the vegetables are tender and lightly charred. Sprinkle with sesame seeds and parsley and toss gently until the vegetables are evenly coated. Serve immediately.

Serves 6–8
Vegetarian

3 tbsp olive oil

900g (2lb) carrots, trimmed, peeled and halved lengthways

900g (2lb) large parsnips, trimmed, peeled, quartered and cored

2 tbsp runny honey

2 tbsp light soy sauce

1 mild red chilli, deseeded and finely chopped

1 tsp toasted sesame seeds

2 tbsp chopped flat-leaf parsley

salt and freshly ground black pepper

Creamy Mashed Potatoes

Delicious mash goes with almost any main course and can be flavoured according to the dish. Choose a floury variety of potato such as Rooster or Maris Piper – if in doubt check the details on the packet before purchasing.

Place the potatoes in a large saucepan of salted water. Bring to the boil, cover and simmer for 15–20 minutes or until the potatoes are tender. Drain and return to the saucepan over a low heat to dry out.

Mash the potatoes or pass through a potato ricer or mouli for a really smooth finish. Heat the butter and milk in a small saucepan until the milk just comes to the boil and the butter has melted. Use a wooden spoon to beat the milk mixture into the mashed potatoes, a little at a time, until the mash is smooth and creamy. Season to taste and serve at once.

Variations

Replace 2 tablespoons of the milk with crème fraîche or cream for a richer version. A couple of tablespoons of snipped chives or a good dollop of Dijon mustard makes a nice addition. Make an olive oil mash by replacing the butter with 6 tablespoons of extra virgin olive oil.

Serves 4–6
Vegetarian

1.5kg (3lb 5oz) floury potatoes, (e.g. Maris Piper or Rooster), cut into even-sized chunks

75g (3oz) butter

about 100ml (4fl oz) milk

salt and freshly ground white pepper

Beef Stock

This takes some time to make but it is worth your while. It is vital to use red wine and tomato purée for real depth of colour. It stores very well in the fridge for 3 days or can be frozen.

Preheat the oven to 220°C (425°F), gas mark 7. Place the shin of beef and marrow bones or knuckle of veal in a roasting tin and cook in the oven for 30–40 minutes until well browned. Drain off all the excess oil and discard. Meanwhile, heat the olive oil in a large saucepan. Add the onion, carrot and celery and sauté for about 6–7 minutes until they are just beginning to colour. Stir in the tomato purée, then pour in the red wine and allow it to bubble down for 1 minute.

Add the roasted meat bones to the vegetable and wine mixture with the garlic and bouquet garni. Season with the salt and pour in 1.75 litres (3 pints) of water. Bring to the boil and skim off any scum, then partially cover and reduce the heat to simmer for 4–5 hours until you have a well-flavoured stock, topping up occasionally with a little water, you'll need to add another 1.2 litres (2 pints) in total over the whole cooking time.

Strain the stock and allow to cool completely before chilling in the fridge. Once cold, remove any trace of solidified fat from the surface with a large spoon, then cover with a lid and return to the fridge until needed. Use as required or freeze in 600ml (1 pint) cartons and thaw when required.

Makes 1.75 litres (3 pints)

700g (1½lb) shin of beef, cut into pieces
700g (1½lb) marrow bones or knuckle of veal, chopped
1 tbsp olive oil
1 onion, peeled and sliced
1 carrot, peeled and sliced
1 celery stick, sliced
1 tbsp tomato purée
150ml (¼ pint) red wine
1 small garlic bulb, halved
1 bouquet garni (parsley stalks, sprigs of thyme and a bay leaf tied together)
½ tsp salt

Vegetable Stock

If time allows, I leave this vegetable stock to marinate for 2 days so that the flavours can really infuse and develop. This gives a much fuller taste and is definitely worth the extra wait!

Place all the ingredients in a large saucepan and cover with 1.75 litres (3 pints) of cold water. Cover with a lid and bring to a simmer, then remove the lid and cook for 30 minutes until the vegetables are tender.

Either set aside to marinate for 2 days in a cool place, or if you're short on time, strain the stock through a sieve. Taste the stock and if you find the flavour is not full enough, return it to the saucepan and reduce it over a medium heat until the required flavour is achieved. Strain the marinated stock through a sieve and use as required or freeze in 600ml (1 pint) cartons, and thaw it when you need it.

Makes 1.2 litres (2 pints)
Vegetarian

2 leeks, trimmed and finely chopped
2 onions, peeled and finely chopped
2 carrots, peeled and cut into 1cm (½in) dice
2 celery sticks, finely chopped
1 fennel bulb, cut into 1cm (½in) dice
1 head of garlic, sliced in half across
1 sprig of thyme
1 fresh bay leaf
1 tsp pink peppercorns
1 tsp coriander seeds
1 star anise
pinch of salt

Chicken Stock

I use chicken stock more than any other type, as it makes the perfect base for soups, stews and sauces. It freezes well so I always have some to hand.

If using a raw chicken carcass, place it in a roasting tin and preheat the oven to 220°C (425°F), gas mark 7. Roast the chicken carcass for about 40 minutes until golden. Drain the chicken in a colander to get rid of any excess fat, then chop it up.

Place the chopped up chicken carcass in a large saucepan and cover it with 1.75 litres (3 pints) of cold water. Bring to the boil, then skim off any fat and scum from the surface. Reduce the heat to a simmer and tip in all the remaining ingredients.

Simmer gently for another 1–1½ hours, skimming occasionally, and top up with water as necessary. Taste regularly to check the flavour. When you're happy with it, remove from the heat and pass through a sieve.

Allow to cool and remove any fat that settles on the top. Use as required or freeze in 600ml (1 pint) cartons, and thaw it when you need it.

Makes 1.2 litres (2 pints)

1 large raw or cooked chicken carcass, skin and fat removed and bones chopped
2 leeks, trimmed and chopped
2 onions, peeled and chopped
2 carrots, peeled and chopped
2 celery sticks, chopped
1 sprig of thyme
1 fresh bay leaf
handful of parsley stalks
1 tsp white peppercorns

Fish Stock

Lemon sole, brill and plaice bones make a wonderful, almost sweet fish stock. It is fine to include heads, bones and skin from most types of fish, but avoid salmon, red mullet and oily fish. Once the stock is made you can reduce it further and then freeze it in ice cube trays (this allows you to thaw as little or as much as you need at a time).

Rinse the fish bones and trimmings of any blood, which would make the stock cloudy and taste bitter. Place in a large, heavy-based saucepan with the leeks, fennel, carrots and parsley. Pour in the wine, then add 2.4 litres (4 pints) of cold water to cover the fish and vegetables. Place over a high heat and bring to a simmer. After 5 minutes, remove the scum that forms on the surface with a spoon and discard. Reduce the heat and simmer, covered, for about 25 minutes, skimming as necessary.

At the end of the cooking time, remove the stock from the heat and strain, discarding the fish trimmings and the vegetables.

Cool and store in the fridge for up to 3 days or freeze in 600ml (1 pint) cartons, and thaw it when you need it.

Makes 1.2 litres (2 pints)

250g (9oz) white fish trimmings and/or bones
3 leeks, trimmed and chopped
1 fennel bulb, chopped
3 carrots, peeled and chopped
large handful of flat-leaf parsley, roughly chopped
175ml (6fl oz) dry white wine

French Vinaigrette

All serious cooks should learn how to make this classic dressing.

Makes about 85ml (3fl oz)
Vegetarian

1 tbsp white wine vinegar
pinch of caster sugar
4 tbsp extra virgin olive oil
½ tsp Dijon mustard
1 small garlic clove, peeled and crushed
salt and freshly ground black pepper

Place the vinegar in a screw-topped jar and add the sugar and a good pinch of salt, then shake until the salt has dissolved.

Add the oil to the jar along with the mustard and garlic and shake again until the ingredients form a thick, blended emulsion. Season with salt and pepper to taste and use as required. Keep in the fridge for up to 1 week.

Variations

Balsamic & Honey Dressing

Replace the white wine vinegar with 2 tablespoons of balsamic vinegar and replace the sugar with ½ teaspoon of runny honey. Omit the Dijon mustard. Makes about 100ml (3½fl oz).

Sherry Dressing

Replace the white wine vinegar with 2 tablespoons of sherry vinegar and use light muscovado sugar instead of caster sugar. Use a teaspoon of wholegrain mustard instead of the Dijon mustard and add a teaspoon of golden syrup. Omit the garlic. Makes about 100ml (3½fl oz).

Index

Acknowledgements

2009 has been the busiest year of my life and more than ever I have benefited from the support of many people in my business and personal life. I will mention just a few.

When you get a good team, stick with it. Once again, Orla Broderick and Sharon Hearne-Smith gave invaluable help compiling and testing recipes. They received great assistance from Zara McHugh who typed everything and from Criona Johnston for proofreading. The team at HarperCollins were again led by the inspired Jenny Heller who first put the idea of *Home Chef* to me. Ione Walder made sure it all happened and was again a joy to work with. Thanks, as always, to Moira Reilly for her PR work. I am thrilled with the photography of David Munns, Nicky Barneby's design work and the cover by Heike Schuessler. Bridget Sargeson worked tirelessly to make the food look stunning, and Sue Rowlands styled the props beautifully. Thanks to Geoff Duke, John Maguire and Helene Seglem for providing us with gorgeous props.

The accompanying television series is again produced and directed by David Hare of InProduction with that wonderful crew of Billy Keady and Ray deBruin. I am grateful to Brian Walsh of RTE for his continued support.

I continue to give demonstrations all around Ireland, at which people ask me the questions that I have tried to answer in this book. I am grateful to Eoin O'Flynn from Flogas, and to Louise Collins and Anna Dawson at VW for providing the car that gets me there and back. My wife, Amelda, makes sure all the arrangements run smoothly.

MacNean House and Restaurant is where my heart is, and there I am surrounded by family and friends. When guests contact us, the first person they speak to is my sister, Suzanne, who looks after reservations. We aim to provide a friendly, relaxed and comfortable atmosphere and this is achieved by Marian, Eileen and Anne in housekeeping and Blaíthín, Jorg and their wonderful front-of-house team.

Then there are the chefs, who all follow the lead of Head Chef, Glen Wheeler. I am so grateful for the hard work and commitment from them all – Declan Greene, Laura Mullen, Vicky Boughton, Zara McHugh, Robert Wilson, Piotr and Pawel Ciesielski, James Devine, Susan Murphy, Criona Johnston and Adrian Martin. They share my passion for food, and this is so essential.

2009 was a difficult year for businesses, so I am grateful to my accountant, Kieran McGovern, for keeping me on track. I am also indebted to my suppliers who never let me down. Thank you to Maurice, Mark and Hugh at Kettyle Irish Foods; Kevin McGovern, my local butcher; Ken Moffitt for free range poultry; and to Peter Curry and Mourne Seafood for fresh seafood. Sakina from Vanilla Bazaar; Norman, Penn and James at Thai Foods; McDaids for their fruit and vegetables; Samantha and Hugh at BD foods; Monaghan; Rod at Eden plants; Ernest at Barbizon Herbs; and Peter and Helena Cumisky who have given me a real love for wine (as well as many a sore head!).

I have greatly enjoyed writing my column in the Farmers' Journal and my thanks to Mairead Lavery and Penny Osborne for making it all happen. I continue to receive much appreciated support from the media and daily help from my publicist, Mary Tallent at Purcell Masterson. Particular thanks to Georgina Campbell, Bairbre Power, Brendan O'Connor, Mary O'Sullivan, Paolo Tullio, Tom Doorly, John & Sally McKenna, Hugo Arnold, Corina Hargreaves, Ross Golden Bannon, Norah Casey and all at Food & Wine, Reg Looby at RTE's *The Restaurant*, and to Anne Farrell and Elaine Conlon and of course Marian Finucane at *The Marian Finucane Show*.

In Blacklion I love meeting the people who come to eat my food. They make the hard work so worthwhile and I hope to always fulfil their expectations. I am also thankful for the daily support from my mother, Vera, and our extended family. And, of course, my wife Amelda. Thank you from the bottom of my heart.